The
Pearly Prince
of
St Pancras

The
Pearly Prince
of
St Pancras

Alf Dole & Jeff Hudson

**SIMON &
SCHUSTER**

London · New York · Sydney · Toronto · New Delhi

A CBS COMPANY

First published in Great Britain by Simon & Schuster UK Ltd, 2014
A CBS COMPANY

1 3 5 7 9 10 8 6 4 2

Simon & Schuster UK Ltd
1st Floor
222 Gray's Inn Road
London WC1X 8HB

www.simonandschuster.co.uk

Simon & Schuster Australia, Sydney
Simon & Schuster India, New Delhi

A CIP catalogue record for this book
is available from the British Library.

Paperback ISBN: 978-1-47113-264-3
Ebook ISBN: 978-1-47113-265-0

Typeset by M Rules
Printed and bound by CPI Group (UK) Ltd, Croydon, CR0 4YY

Contents

A Few Words From Suggs

This is a fascinating and original story of one of the last true pearly kings, Alf Dole, Pearly King of St Pancras, who could trace his family roots back to the costermongers. The pearly attitude to life is one of pride, not just to raise money for the needy but also to dispense the true cockney spirit, which Alf always did in his pearly button taxi with the radio up loud, blasting out cockney songs and getting everybody to join in. And of course he played the spoons whenever he could, including on stage with Madness when we did a London show. He could be found most Sundays at Greenwich in his taxi collecting for his favourite charity, Great Ormond Street Hospital. Alf . . . a true pearly legend!

Suggs
April 2014

Prologue

I'll Get My Own Drinks

The two cars were a write-off. I could make that much out. When I went closer I saw one of the drivers had his hands round the throat of the other. Two passers-by pulled him off but he kept trying to go back to land a punch.

'What the hell were you playing at?'

'I told you, mate, I didn't see you.'

'How can you not see me? Look at the size of my car.'

The other guy laughed.

'Are you serious? I can only see you now because you're a foot in front of me.'

Eventually they both calmed down and agreed it was neither driver's fault. Not really.

'This bloody war,' one of them said. 'This blackout will kill us before Hitler does.'

You took your life in your own hands walking along the Euston Road at night in 1940. There were no street lamps, all windows of the houses and pubs along the route were boarded up and the cars and buses had to pick their way without headlights. They should have slowed down but most didn't, and as pedestrians you needed your wits to avoid vehicles coming out of nowhere and mounting the pavement on a bend. Not a night passed without a collision of some sort. In the mornings I'd find telltale bits of bumper or headlamp glass as I walked into town.

It was safer when you turned off the main road but no lighter. Cars rarely ventured up Chalton Street and no one living in Somers Town could afford much more than a horse and cart. Shanks's pony did most of us just fine. For the rest there were the trams, the new trolleybuses or the underground.

I was heading to Charrington Street and I was late. I'd been out with mates and promised Mum I'd be home by nine. It must have been nearly eleven. The only hope I had was if she was out as well. And, if she was, I had a pretty good idea where she'd be. It was Saturday, after all.

I could hear the Eastnor Castle before I could see it. Sixty or seventy voices were singing and somewhere, drowned in the chorus, was a piano struggling to be heard. I made my way over to where men were standing outside, smoking. Not because of the law like today, but because it was so hot inside. They all had smiles on their faces.

'All right, Alfie?' one of them, the local haberdasher, called out when he spotted me.

'Hi, Mr Jacobs. Is my mum in there?'

'You're in luck,' he laughed. 'She's over the back. If you get home now she'll be none the wiser.'

I didn't answer that. How did he know what I was thinking?

'I was young once, you know.'

I was about to take his advice and run home when I realised the music had stopped and the singing with it. There was just one voice coming from inside the pub now and he had everyone in stitches. I knew it was risky, but I had to have a look.

I pushed past Mr Jacobs and stood outside the doors. They were wooden with boarded windows, like everywhere else. Even if they weren't I probably couldn't have seen through the frosted glass. There was only one way to see what was going on inside.

I pushed the right-hand door open and met a wall of bodies with their backs to me. That was a relief. It meant Mum couldn't see me. On the other hand, I couldn't see in. I was ten years old and not tall for my age; just over waist height of most of the people there. Spying a gap between a man and woman, I squeezed through then stopped.

Everyone in the saloon was in stitches at the man in the middle of the room. He was telling a story that went off in this direction and that, getting more preposterous by the minute. At every turn a couple of drinkers would heckle him with insults and he'd just bat them away with another joke. When he finished – finally – he got a round of applause and the people on the edges stepped forwards to slap him on the shoulder and offer to buy him a drink. As they got near him, he produced a metal box and waved it under their noses.

'I'll get my own drinks, thanks, but you can put the price of an ale in the tin if you don't mind.'

They all did. I watched as the man went round the pub, slowly, chatting to everyone, and encouraging them all to dig deep and drop a penny or two into his collection tin. It was no mean feat. We were a country at war. There was rationing and people had already been poor to start with. But most drinkers gave because they understood every penny would end up helping a good cause. The man didn't have to tell them – they knew from what he was wearing. His suit, covered top to bottom in sparkling white mother-of-pearl buttons, was his calling card.

I realised I'd stood there too long when the man shook his tin at the couple I was hiding behind and said, 'It's a bit late for you, Alfie, isn't it?'

'Sorry, Granddad,' I said. 'I wanted to hear your story.'

He laughed. 'You've heard it before. You've heard them all before!'

He was probably right. There was nothing I loved more than listening to my granddad spin his yarns, with or without his suit. But watching him perform, all dressed up, in front of a large audience was a thrill that was worth getting a telling off for.

'Your mum's heading home soon,' he said. 'I suggest you're there before she is.'

He was right. It must have been near closing time. I ran back out, across Chalton Street, round the school at the top of the road and down Charrington. I fished the key to our house through the letterbox and let myself in. The house was cold and dark but I was warm as toast on adrenaline and pride. I was never happier than watching Granddad strut his stuff in public. It was worth a clout from Mum to see him in action because if there was anyone in the world I wanted to be like, it was him.

I climbed into bed next to my younger brother and closed my eyes, praying for the same thing I wished for every night.

'Dear God, please let me be one. Please let me be a Pearly King.'

I

Give Us an Apple, Mr Dole

In the beginning there was fruit – and the fruit was good. Bloomin' good, actually, and in plentiful supply. That's the benefit of having a greengrocer as the head of the family. To be honest, even when the fruit wasn't as box fresh as it might have been, it found its way into pies or tarts or drinks somehow. And if there was a profit to be turned, then you could rely on him to find the way.

George Dole was the man with his name above the shop at 151 Chalton Street, NW1. To me he was 'Granddad', to his customers he was 'George' or 'Mr Dole'. But to the barrow boys, costermongers and importers down at Covent Garden fruit market he was known by a different name: 'Specky' – and it was nothing to do with him wearing glasses.

With so much fruit coming into London from all over the world before the war, the greengrocers could afford to be picky and wholesalers were kept on their toes to compete with each other. If you sold a bad lot to a greengrocer one week, he'd go to one of your competitors next time. So before anything was sold, each piece of fruit and veg would be gone through and any that hadn't survived the trip from the West Indies or Holland or the south of England would be tossed out. Oranges, for example, were prone to getting little 'specks' on them when they started to turn. Any found with the giveaway white marks would be thrown into the big bins round the back of the stalls.

And that's where Granddad would be waiting.

He'd sort through the runts, load them onto his barrow with all the healthy-looking produce for the week, then take it back to the shop. Then, that night, he'd go through the oranges, scraping off all the specks with a knife; he'd give them a wash, and he'd be left with a few pounds of 'good as new' Jaffas. Of course, he wouldn't sell them in his shop – he had a reputation to think of! – but Sundays were different. Shops weren't allowed to open on the Lord's Day, but Granddad didn't see why the government should dictate when people could buy fruit, so he'd send his son – my uncle – Jim out with a barrow and flog the oranges for a penny. Everyone wins.

In truth, George earned enough from his shop that he didn't need to be selling salvage satsumas on his day off. But it was habit. He hadn't always had premises. He'd started out with a barrow in 1895 and would walk up and down the streets hawking his wares alongside a dozen or more other traders, many of them flogging the same fruit from the same market at the same prices. All sorts of things were sold from barrows but the men – and boys – who sold fruit were called costermongers. 'Coster' comes from an old type of apple called a 'costard'; and 'monger' means seller, hence the name. You can't watch an old film set in London without seeing them in the background, usually singing and dancing behind the likes of Mary Poppins or Eliza Doolittle. But anyone thinking it was a romantic life has never tried selling browned fruit in the November rain. The competition was so great and the profit margin so slim that a day of bad weather could seriously dent a man's income. Two days would put him in trouble with the rent man. Anything above three and he probably wouldn't be able to feed himself or his family – or afford to buy new stock when the current crop perished. A lot of costers were driven to all sorts of tricks to con their customers for more profit. Some hollowed out the weights on their scales so a pound of apples was closer to half. Some hid the bad fruit at the bottom of the bags. And some earned more from picking the pockets of passers-by than by selling anything.

It was brutal, dog-eat-dog, and it convinced Granddad that he needed to get a roof over his head. But he never stopped being a coster at heart, even when he did acquire No. 151 Chalton Street. If a seller was in trouble with the police, Granddad would hide him or his barrow and send the copper then the coster on his way – no questions asked. When the winter weather hit, he was one of the first to hand out food to starving coster families or to start a whip-round to tide them over. More than once he confronted landlords to stop costers being evicted and, when that didn't work, took in entire families until they got back on their feet. He wasn't the only one, but he had more to offer than most.

It was partly because Granddad's days of selling fruit from

a barrow were behind him that he sent Uncle Jim out on a Sunday. But there was another reason for not doing it himself. First thing Sundays he'd be down to Billingsgate and buy a crate of eels fresh from the Thames and cockles, whelks and whatever else had come in on the trawlers overnight. Then he'd pitch up outside the Eastnor Castle pub just along from his shop and feed all the customers out for a Sunday pint. And if he happened to spend most of his earnings in the pub that night, so be it.

But it wasn't just the fruit that Granddad wouldn't let go to waste, as I discovered when I was asked to do my bit to help my parents move house.

'Why do we need this old thing?' I said, kicking the decrepit crate I'd been told to carry downstairs. 'Granddad's got loads in his shop.'

The crate was about two foot long by fifteen inches across and made of smooth, soft wood, like ply. On each side there was one word, stencilled on in black ink: 'Jaffa'. The oranges had long been taken out. Instead it was half-filled with sheets and a couple of coloured scarves.

'Well, you're an unsentimental devil, aren't you,' Mum laughed from behind the stack of grey bedding she was folding.

I shrugged. I was five years old and desperate to get out of helping. I'd already packed hairbrushes, shoes and anything else that didn't look too heavy. This crate was light but cumbersome. I didn't fancy lugging it down the threadbare stairs. There were enough adults with Dad and his brothers buzzing in and out and, in any case, I wanted to be outside with my mates.

'What's so special about an old crate?' I asked.

'That old crate, as you call it, used to be your bed. You were happy enough with it as a baby.'

I looked at the splintered slats poking out from beneath the pile of linen and scarves. It didn't look comfy. I wasn't even sure it looked safe. Still, it did explain why I remembered liking the smell of oranges so much.

'Why didn't I have a cot, Mum?' I asked.

Now it was her turn to shrug.

'Cots cost money and, as you rightly say, your granddad has plenty of these crates.'

She put down her bedding, came over to the crate and picked up one of the sheets. I'd never seen my mother cry before but I was worried that was about to change.

'So I had a wooden box instead of a cot?'

Mum nodded.

'Wow,' I said. 'Like Jesus.'

Now she just laughed. 'Well,' she said, 'I think Jesus's box was a manger, love, but I suppose it's near enough.'

Then she put the sheet back, lifted the whole thing into my arms and told me to skedaddle. Which I did, taking our little terrier, Rags, with me. Down to the front door, out into the street, and up onto the barrow already loaded with our stuff.

So, there you go. My earliest memory is of me discovering my parents couldn't afford a proper baby bed – and comparing myself to the Son of God in the process.

Aim high, that's me!

*

I may not have been Jesus but my mum's name was Mary and, on 14 January 1930, she popped me out into the world, right there facing Euston Station in Bridgeway Street, with the help of a neighbour called Pol Sharpe. What Mrs Sharpe lacked in medical qualifications she made up for in experience. Half the kids in the area known as Somers Town were born to the sound of Pol calling out, 'Push!' to their frightened young mums. Sometimes I used to see her in the street and she'd give me a wave or, if I was with friends, stop to embarrass me about how she'd seen my little pink bum. Other times she wouldn't return my 'hello', she'd just stare at the floor on her way past.

'Someone hasn't been so lucky as us today,' Mum would say. When I asked what she meant she wouldn't explain. As I grew older I realised that Mrs Sharpe could only do so much with her warm water and towels heated by the fire. If anything went wrong during a labour no one had a telephone and even though the Elizabeth Garrett Anderson maternity hospital was just off the Euston Road, getting there in time was usually a journey too far for some little 'un or their mum. Sometimes both.

When you look at it like that, what's the big deal about sleeping in a packing crate from the West Indies? At least it was mine. And if I ever did get a splinter it was coated in so much juice it was probably like getting a shot of vitamin C. What could be healthier than that?

Speaking of health, Mum used to love having the windows open. With the wind in the right direction we could hear the steam trains running in and out. Between Euston on one side and St Pancras main line on the other, some hot days the smell of burning coal in the air made it feel like winter. At other times the only thing filling your nostrils was the stench of horses from the carts making their way to Eversholt Street at one end of the street or Chalton Street at the other. Where there's horses, there's dung. Sometimes I couldn't breathe for the pen 'n' ink (*stink*) outside the front door.

Eversholt Street was called Seymour Road back then, like Chalton was signposted Stibbington before I was born. I don't know why they were changed but they stank as bad, whatever they were called.

'Fresh' was how Mum used to describe it. 'Bloody disgusting' was my opinion – although I got a whack if she ever heard me say that. Granddad just used to laugh. But then half the time the pong came from his horses – or ponies. He had a couple that he kept in stables in Camley Mews round the back of St Pancras.

Chalton Street was just a couple of stone-throws away from us – wherever we lived. I was born on Bridgeway Street, which comes off Chalton, but by the time I found the orange crate we were living on Medburn Street. The only thing between us and Granddad's shop was the big old secondary school. At playtimes Granddad would hear the kids calling out, 'Give us an apple, Mr Dole!' He'd go over or send Jim with a boxful and charge them a penny a go. He sold just as many to the teachers – but he charged them tuppence.

The school's still there but it's a college now and almost double in size. Whatever the kids do in playtime, they don't call out to the greengrocer opposite – No. 151 and all the shops around it were replaced by a council block in the 1960s. There aren't any shops at all at the top end of Chalton Street any more. It's a bit soulless, if you ask me. Where's the community supposed to gather and meet and have a chat about each other's lives? You have to go down as far as Phoenix Road before you can spend your money anywhere. Chalton Street used to have a butcher's, a baker's, a haberdasher's – all the essentials. Now there's a 'Fruit Juice and Electric Cigarette Bar' opposite the market.

But that's now. When I was growing up there was a real buzz to our little patch of Somers Town and, at the heart of it, more often than not, was Granddad George. Whether you saw him riding his cart down to market or hawking his wares outside his shop on Chalton Street, he had a way with words that made you stop and listen. I would see people cross the road to talk to him and more often than not they'd end up buying something. But it didn't matter to him whether you were a customer or a passer-by. He had a 'hello', a 'good morning' and usually a story for everyone.

Anyone who ever met George Dole remembered him. It wasn't just what he said that made him stand out. It was the way he said it, as well. Apart from an Italian family and a couple of Jewish households, his shop at No. 151 was the only place in the area you'd hear an accent that wasn't London-born. George and his wife Emma had come over from Dublin in 1894 and, while they left a lot of things behind, their accents were definitely not one of them.

It wasn't just the way he sounded that gave Granddad away as a son of the Emerald Isle. The way he talked – and talked, and talked . . . and *talked* – left everyone who heard him in no doubt he'd hadn't just kissed the Blarney Stone, he'd swallowed it. No one ever popped into his shop if they were in a hurry. And they never left without a smile to go with their fruit 'n' veg, either.

Over the years all manner of accents blended into the area, like everywhere else in London. I remember when we used to call Clerkenwell 'Little Italy' because of the new-wave Roman invasion going on there. In the beginning, though, it was just the odd family who'd opted to see the world for whatever reason and the occasional sailor who'd jumped ship down at East India Docks and decided to chance his luck a bit further north where the dockyard guards wouldn't spot him. It was a real melting pot down by the Thames, so the visitors thought all London was cosmopolitan like that. But the second the newcomers moved away from the river they stood out as soon as they opened their north and south.

I remember seeing a couple of rozzers march a bloke out of a flat on Ossulston Street once. The poor guy was holding his trousers up with one hand and carrying his shirt and coat in the other, so I could see the tattoos up his arms. Apparently he'd scarpered from a Polish boat a couple of months earlier to be with a woman he'd met in a pub. A lot of them did that. Being at sea so long made them reckless. On the outside he looked as English as you and me. It wasn't a bad disguise, I suppose, until he had to speak. Then his goose was well and truly cooked.

You could stroll round Camden Market or Chalk Farm all day without hearing anything but 'London' voices. Just occasionally, though, you'd spin round to see who had the exotic way with words. It might be a woman arguing with a butcher in broken English and hand signals or a man in a suit buying something nice for his wife. It was rare enough to make you look.

Granddad George took everyone he met at face value. Regardless of whether he could understand them or not, he made sure they understood him.

'It doesn't matter where in the world you are from, a man needs to eat fruit.' And as long as that was the case, he was happy.

Eighty or so years later it's a lesson I'm proud to have lived by – apart from the fruit bit. I can't offer anyone that, but I can show them a giggle and that, I promise, is an international language in itself.

While no one who ever met him was in any doubt, on paper 'George Dole' doesn't seem particularly Irish – but then George Dole was not the name Granddad left home with. He was christened George 'Doyle', from a long, long line of Doyles, and, like every Irishman, he was incredibly proud of his heritage. What he wasn't, however, was eagle-eyed. When he signed all the papers for residency in England back in 1894 he didn't spot that his name had been written 'Dole'. Once the government decides that's your name, then it's best to stick with it. That was George's point of view, anyway. And, as he told me, 'It was a fresh beginning so a fresh name didn't hurt. But nobody was in any doubt where we were from!'

Years later there was a US senator called Bob Dole, who ran for the White House at one point. I dropped him a line a while ago to ask if his grandfather had mislaid a 'Y' anywhere along the line. You never know, we might be related!

There I go, aiming high again, but in all seriousness it wasn't a totally fanciful notion to wonder if Bob Dole came from the same line as me, because there were plenty who did. Obviously there was no TV back in 1894 nor, as far as I can tell, much else in the way of entertainment. How else do you explain that Granddad and Grandma went on to have seventeen children? And that's just the ones I know of (by which I mean the ones who survived). That generation's Mrs Sharpe was kept busy. It's almost like they were making up for the family they'd left behind in Ireland. Whatever the reason, within a generation there were suddenly more Doles in north London than a lot of other, more established, names. And of course, there were some I never ever met. Who's to say they never ended up running for office in Kansas?

Plenty of aunties, uncles and cousins I did meet, however, and in fact spent a lot of time with. Jim, Walter, Mike, Katie, Joan, Dolly, Maureen, Patsy, Lana, Dave, Annie, Polly, George, Bill – and that's barely half of them – were regular faces when I was growing up, popping in and out of our lives from time to time like customers popping in and out of Granddad's shop. Keeping in touch with people, even relatives, wasn't as straightforward then as it is now. There weren't emails, cars or even telephones, not for the likes of us. If you didn't live within a couple of streets of each other you were pretty much off the radar.

More often than not, though, I saw most of the Dole line at the various family functions when they turned up with their own families. All except Uncle Patsy. He never married and, as far as I remember, he never left home, either. Weirdly, he kept pets that did exactly the same. A lot of the men in my family loved racing pigeons but Patsy was the keenest. He converted the attic at No. 151 into a pigeon loft and he loved those birds like they were his children. You could eat a meal off the floor of that attic. It was cleaned every day, the birds were fed and watered to schedule and when they went out for fresh air or to race, Uncle Patsy could not relax until each one was counted home. I don't know who had the biggest homing instinct: him or his birds.

Granddad loved the pigeons too, but, like several of his other lads, he enjoyed them more for the chance to have a flutter on their results. It was Patsy who was in it for the love of the animals. He was the proper fancier. He did all the grooming and the breeding and it was one of his birds that won the longest distance race in the UK. The bird got a little extra millet in its feed that night and Granddad went home very happy because he'd put a few quid on the result. Patsy was just glad to see the bird home in one piece. One of my earliest memories is going up into the attic to see all the little birds in their cages. The smell wasn't far off the horse pong outside our house, but the noise was something else. There must have been about two or three dozen little grey things and individually they just cooed and gobbled and clucked. Together, though, they made a sound like a drill coming through the roof. Uncle Patsy loved that.

'They're saying they're not sure about you,' he explained, a glint in his eye at my fear. 'Do you want me to let them out?'

'Er, no, you're all right, Uncle Patsy.'

He laughed.

'I'm only kidding, son. They're just hungry, that's all.'

'Phew.'

Then he leaned in. 'What do you think I should feed them? They're partial to little boys.'

That was it. I flew out of the attic down to the back room. Granddad was just sitting down with a glass.

'The pigeons are after me!' I said.

'You tell them they'll taste nice with a few carrots and bit of potato mash,' he said. 'I've got some in the shop.'

I crept back up to the attic and told Uncle Patsy I was going to cook his precious birds if they tried to peck me. He threw me out and never teased me again.

I would never have hurt the birds, of course, and Uncle Patsy knew it. But when you were raised with the number of brothers he was, I can't blame him for being careful.

Of all George and Emma's kids, there were two I was closer to than the others. Annie and Alfred weren't the oldest and they weren't the youngest either, but they would always be the same age as each other because they were born twins. In fact they were one of three pairs, which meant Grandma only had to go through fourteen pregnancies. *Only* . . .

All the kids were close but the twins looked out for each other more than the rest. So, when Alf met a young woman called Mary in 1922 Annie couldn't have been happier. When Mary gave birth to a son a couple of years later, it was a different story, because Alf and Mary weren't married. When you've got Irish Catholic parents breathing down your neck, this is not the way to go. Obviously Granddad was not one to preach about contraception but he was furious Alf couldn't have waited, especially as he and Mary split up soon after. Even the fact the boy was called 'George' in Granddad's honour didn't placate him.

'There'll be no more Doles out of wedlock,' he instructed. 'You make sure you marry the next one.'

Alf was as good as his word – although the 'next one', another Mary, as it happens, came with her own ready-made history. Maybe that was what attracted the pair of them. It certainly wasn't convenience. Mary Dance came from a Romany family that had settled over in Poplar in the East End. With her rich black hair and quick tongue she was a prize Alf could not resist, even when it meant him walking, more often than not, all the way from Somers Town down to Poplar just to see her. Rarely did he have the money for a bus or a train. If he did, he put that aside for when he went out with Mary. If it was just him, it was Shanks's pony all the way.

Alf and Mary had a lot in common, right down to children from previous relationships. Just as George lived with his mum, Mary's son, David, had stayed with her. If Alf wanted to pursue his relationship with Mary, he had to understand he was getting a complete package.

'Are you up for that, Alfred Dole?' Mary asked.

'The more the merrier!'

They were married in 1928 and it wasn't long until they were asking to borrow a Jaffa box in preparation for my arrival on 14 January 1930 – yes, Alf was my dad. It wasn't just money that was scarce, though. Imagination didn't seem in great supply either, especially when it came to giving me a name. I think, if he could, Dad would have named me 'George' after his father, but his first son had already taken that name. Uninspired by all his brothers' monikers, he went for another familiar name:

'Alfred'. Mum obviously didn't see any problem with having two Alfs around the house, although by the time I was old enough to speak I think they all regretted it because I was known as 'Boy-Boy' throughout the family. I asked my mum why no one used my real name.

'It's confusing having two Alfs around the place.'

It's a fair point. Which does somewhat beg the question . . .

If Dad had shown a distinct lack of imagination with my first name, when it got to giving me a middle name he was ahead of his time. I'm not saying the Emirates Stadium up the road from us got the idea from him, but Dad was selling naming rights long before Arsenal got into the game. The only difference was, he wasn't naming a football ground. He was naming me.

It started at work. Dad's trade was as a painter and decorator. Sometimes he temped on building sites for extra money. It was doing a job alongside a Russian guy called Boris and telling him that Mary was expecting that led to an interesting conversation – and a proposal.

'In my country it's customary to give presents when there's a new baby,' Boris explained. 'I'm going to buy the baby's first little suit.'

'That's very kind of you, Boris,' Dad said, 'but I can't let you do that.'

'I insist.'

But Dad wouldn't have it. He was poor but he was proud. If he couldn't afford to buy me new things then he didn't want hand-outs from workmates, especially ones who'd probably had to jump off a ship just to enter the country.

'Okay, we make deal,' Boris said. 'Back home we have a great military general called Avory. If you name your baby after him, I'll buy the suit. It's trade, not gift.'

That sounded better.

'Avory?' Dad repeated, over and over. 'I like it, Boris. You've got a deal.'

'*Spasiba!*' Boris roared. 'Thank you, Alfred.'

Mum was furious that Dad had signed my name away like that, over a handshake with a bloke from a building site.

'You're a fool, Alfred Dole. He won't keep his side, you barely know him. No one gives away money like that. We're gonna saddle the boy with a stupid name for nothing.'

But Boris was as good as his word. No sooner had Pol Sharpe dragged me into the world than the proud-looking Russian arrived with a little knitted outfit of cardigan, trousers and tiny boots, all for me. Mum couldn't get over it. It was the only new thing I ever owned. Who cared about a silly middle name when you had new wool to hold?

And so that's me, Alfred Avory Dole. I've got the same first name as my dad, an obscure Russian general in the middle and basically little more than a typing mistake at the end.

What could go wrong with a start in life like that?

2

If It Wasn't For The
'Ouses In Between

I've always loved the sound of music. Not the 'Do Re Mi' musical kind – that hadn't been made yet. In fact, Julie Andrews herself was just a twinkle in her parents' eyes. The sound of music I'm talking about is the type that, along with the singing and laughing, poured from the open windows of that flat above the greengrocer's shop at 151 Chalton Street.

On a still night you could hear the noise streets away. Men popping along for a pint of bitter next door at the Eastnor Castle would do a double-take at the saloon doors. You could see them thinking, *Where's that party if it's not here?*

But I knew. And I couldn't wait to get up there. Even as a kid too shy to join in, I just loved being part of it. Nobody ever had a bad time in the back room of No. 151.

I remember going round there. Me, David and Mum were waiting for Dad to get home from work. Or it might have been from the pub, as it was Saturday and Mum didn't look too impressed waiting for him. Either way, the second we heard the front door swing open, we were out of our chairs and marching past him before he'd set foot in the house. Dad just shrugged, pulled the door to and fell in line.

Granddad's shop was on Chalton Street but the entrance to the house, if you didn't want to go in past the veg, was round the corner on Cranleigh Street. Mum pushed open the door – like ours, it was rarely locked – and we filed up the stairs. Coming in from outside the first thing that hit me was the smoke. The air outside wasn't exactly fresh, what with all the horse mess, the smell of bins outside some of the blocks and, if the wind was blowing in the right direction, the burned aromas of coal wafting over from the steam trains stoking up at Euston. But stepping into No. 151, you could actually *see* the smells you were breathing in. Everyone had a pipe or a roll-up of Golden Virginia, including the women. I don't remember seeing many ash trays but my aunts and uncles never seemed to need them because the fags seldom appeared to be out of their mouths. I was mesmerised by how Bill, Jim, Dolly and the rest would leave a roll-up on their lips and just continue like it wasn't there. They'd chat away, laugh, even sing, all out of the corner of their mouths, like Popeye. And those little white sticks would flip up and down like they were conducting the Royal Philharmonic, and never ever fall out.

Smoking was seen as a bit glamorous, a bit 'American'. Doctors even said it was good for you. Even the coughing, which Dad managed to get through without pulling a butt out of his mouth, was just one of those things. It definitely didn't put me off.

I've got to try one of these things to see what all the fuss is about.

If anyone would have let me have a puff, it would have been Granddad. As far as tobacco went, however, his preferred method of intake was snuff. He had a little silver box which he kept in his waistcoat or, if he was working, in the pocket of his long, beige greengrocer's coat. Being only waist height to the adults, I got a weird view. I'd watch him talking to someone, then see a hand dart inside and pull out the box. I knew what was coming next. He'd get a pinch of the funny burned leaves inside, bring his hand to his nose and sniff. My God, did he sniff. For a second it looked like his eyes were going to pop out of his head. Then he'd shake his head, just slightly, like a dog, and continue talking like nothing had happened. I'd see the little box returned to the pocket, Granddad would pat his waistcoat absent-mindedly to check it was in place and move on, until the next time.

Being so small there was the danger of falling ash, especially if a group of grown-ups were standing around me. Usually I didn't notice. I'd just feel a rough hand dusting off the top of my head every so often and guess something must have landed there. All I really knew, even as a five-year-old, is that I wanted to try it out for myself.

The room itself, when the fog cleared, was a decent size for a family. Twenty or thirty people packed it out. The walls were papered in brown stripes and there were pictures of the various strands of the family – Grandma, Aunt Anne, even Grandma's own sisters – dotted around. All the women had the same pose and the same sort of formal outfit, with a hat, in those snaps. It was like a series of school photos for grown-ups.

Electricity wasn't everywhere in the country in 1935 but Granddad was plumbed into the mains. A single bulb dangled down from the centre of the high ceiling. On a summer's night I'd sit watching the moths buzz in through the open windows and start head-butting the hot glass. I remember asking Granddad why they did it.

'The moths think it's the moon.'

'But the moon's outside. Look, you can see it.'

'Well,' he shrugged, 'then I guess this must just be closer.'

But on party night you couldn't spot a moth for smoke and you couldn't hear them flutter and crash either. Music filled the room. It filled the house and spilled out along the street, and all without a record player or radio in sight.

Everyone played something. Uncle Paddy would be there on an upturned crate playing the piano. Uncle Wally would have his accordion out. Someone else would be on the banjo, or the tissue paper or the spoons. To this day that's my instrument. You hum it, I can rattle it out on the cutlery. And that's the place, the very room, where I learned to do it.

There were songs for every occasion but everyone had their own favourites that they'd knock out. Granddad did a marvellous turn of an old music hall number, 'If It Wasn't For The 'Ouses In Between'. Apart from kids' rhymes, this was the first time I really listened to the words of a song and when I did they had me in fits of giggles. It's about a man who lived in a built-up place, much like we did, but who thought it was a great location because he could see from Hackney Marshes to Wembley 'if it wasn't for the 'ouses in between'. It didn't matter how many times I heard the lines, they still made me smile. And even when I knew the lyrics off by heart, the way Granddad performed it with his mimes and his puffed-out chest and funny faces kept me in stitches.

Years later Roy Hudd started singing the song in his variety act. It was good, but it wasn't Granddad good. Of course, I didn't tell him that when we met in the 1980s.

Dad wasn't the keenest singer in the room but he could be persuaded. 'It's A Long Way To Tipperary' was one of his favourites, and he'd put on an Irish accent to mimic his dad. Some of his brothers and sisters weren't so shy. I remember some cracking versions of 'Any Old Iron', 'Where Did You Get That Hat' and 'Boiled Beef And Carrots'. It was like having a music hall in your own home.

When it came to performing I was closer to my dad than my granddad. As a five- or six-year-old I hated being dragged up to dance with my mum or nan or aunties. Standing on my own in the corner I'd be more likely to tap my foot and try to clap along. But as soon as a (usually) drunken woman came laughing towards me with her arms outstretched I'd bolt for the door.

When the coast was clear I'd sneak back in, even though there were usually other kids playing elsewhere in the house. With sixteen aunts and uncles I had no shortage of cousins. Boy or girl, most of them preferred to hang out together in Grandma's bedroom or, on summer evenings, outside in the yard or in the street. I was the only one who wanted to stay at the party. The problem was, I loved tearing up and down with my cousins as well, so I'd try to do both.

At least I could hear the music and the sing-songs from outside. When they stopped, that was usually my cue to pelt it back in. Sometimes the quiet meant everyone was tired or they were having a bite to eat – but sometimes it meant it was time for a story. And I loved a story.

I didn't realise it at the time, but what a family of show-offs I came from! Dad or my uncles or Granddad would take the stage and tell a yarn and we'd all sit or stand around listening. My grandma had heard every tale a dozen times or more. A lot of them weren't new to me, either. But it was like with the songs, I just loved hearing them, even when I knew what was coming next. I would stand in the corner or, if there was room, lie there on the rug on my tummy, rapt, my chin in my hands, drinking in the words.

There was something instinctive about it, I could feel it even then. This was the old way of doing things, going back to the ancient Greeks, to Socrates and Plato, just connecting with other people, other family and friends. This was history in the making. History being passed down from generation to generation. But not to me. This wasn't history for me. These were adventure stories – with the people I loved most in the starring roles.

Pretty much every anecdote I heard about my granddad came from his own mouth – usually with the odd 'helpful' reminder from his wife. Grandma loved to puncture his narratives with a correction here, an additional slice of information there. Sometimes there was even a sly dig at him. Quite a lot of the time, actually.

Granddad didn't care. He would rattle on through his story, looking you straight in the eye, painting his picture with words, carrying you on a journey so realistic you felt the story was about you. It didn't matter how many other people were in the room, if he saw me listening he always made me feel like it was just him and me.

I enjoyed Granddad's stories at his parties so much that sometimes I was allowed to creep into the Eastnor Castle or the Neptune or one of the other pubs on Chalton Street and watch as he went round the room spinning a tale for the couples or groups of pals drinking there. Often I wasn't close enough to make out what he was saying over the racket of general conversation, but I could see in his audience's eyes the effect it was having. It was exactly the same effect as he regularly had on me at No. 151, exactly the same performance. But with one difference.

His clothes.

Granddad wore many different hats, and plenty of different suits. But one hat and suit stood out. Because, while he was 'Granddad' to me, 'Specky' to the barrow boys at Covent Garden and 'Mr Dole' to the kids at Medburn Secondary, there was another name that was synonymous with him throughout the borough:

The Pearly King of St Pancras.

3

You Were There

Plenty has been written and said about the origins of the Pearly movement over the years, a lot of it from people who were never there and didn't know anyone who was. They'll all have their own reasons for spinning a yarn, of course, and I'm not going to judge. But George Dole was there at the beginning. In fact, he *was* the beginning. He might not have been the first man to pull on the buttons but he knew the man who did.

Henry Croft grew up in a workhouse in Charles Street (now Phoenix Road), Somers Town. By the age of thirteen he was considered an adult and expected to find his own way in the world. Fortunately, Camden borough council considered him old enough to employ, and so the young teenager became an official road sweeper for the area.

Part of his patch was Somers Town and, in particular, the long streets leading north from Euston Road. He spent most of his time clearing up the mess left by the markets, the costers and the hawkers – which is why it's odd that he developed such a fascination for those men and women who earned their crust selling in the street. Put it this way, they wouldn't have been on my Christmas card list if I had to clean up after them.

But Henry saw more than the brown bags and squashed apples littering the floor. He saw a real community among all the men and women who, on the face of it, were competing against each other for every single penny they could charm out of the passing trade. According to the stories that Granddad used to tell, Henry couldn't get over how the costers might have a scrap among themselves one minute but they all pulled together the next if one of them was in trouble. Forget all the tales of gangsters being hard men but fair – the costers were the originals. Even the police thought twice about taking them on because they knew hundreds more would appear out of the woodwork if they did.

There was something else about the costers that Henry liked. Most of them wore a version of the 'uniform' that had been passed down through the centuries, from the times of Shakespeare – a cravat, a hat and a dark brown suit, augmented by a row of buttons running up the trouser leg or around the breast pocket. Even though the costers were poor, it was important to them to show that they were united. It was a symbol, more than anything, they weren't just a random group of men and women. They were a family.

As an orphan this struck a chord with Henry. And as a good soul, he knew he wanted to do something to help the place that had raised him. But collecting money was the work of the church – who would hand over two bob to a road sweeper?

Months and years went by and Henry pondered what he could do. But times were hard for him and he had a crust to earn in all weathers, just like the street vendors. And then one day he had a stroke of luck.

According to Granddad, Henry was walking down by the Thames when he found a large box, like a trunk, washed up on the shore. It didn't take much to crack the lock open. Whatever he was expecting to find, he knew it would almost certainly have been ruined by the water. What he found, however, was not only waterproof but it gave him an idea.

The trunk was filled with white mother-of-pearl oyster shell buttons.

It seemed like a sign. Over the next weeks and months Henry found a suit and taught himself to sew the buttons on. He started cautiously at first, mimicking the pattern that he'd seen on the costers' uniforms. Then, proud of his handiwork, he added another line to the seams of the jacket, then another, then another. Eventually he had covered all the fabric, with plenty of buttons left.

That's Granddad's version of events, anyway. Other people have said that Henry bought the buttons at a haberdashers and made up the story to people like George Dole to inspire them. Either way, it was the same result, but I know which account I believe.

Regardless of how he acquired his buttons, taking his first steps outside the dingy room he shared in Eversholt Street, I can imagine Henry having second thoughts. He'd set out to pay trib-ute to the costermongers, but would they just think he was taking the mickey? He'd seen what they could do with their fists. He'd also seen how many of them there were.

Maybe he should just go back inside . . .?

But Henry was still a teenager full of the impetuosity of youth. He'd lost track of how many times he'd drawn blood with his sewing needle. He was damned if all that blood, sweat and tears was going to go to waste.

Of course, he was an instant hit. More than that, he was a hero. When he said he wanted to raise money for the orphanage, every person who heard him dug their hand into their pocket. And the ones who couldn't afford anything said, 'The next apple I sell is going to you, Henry.'

When he turned up at Charles Street with nearly a pound in donations, and saw the faces on the staff there, he felt like a king.

A Pearly King.

Over the next few years Henry became known all over the borough as the Pearly King of Somers Town. When George Dole arrived and set up shop, the two became fast friends, with Henry a regular, almost daily, visitor to No. 151. He'd always get a cup of tea and an orange – specky or otherwise – if he popped his head through the door, he knew that. In Granddad, Henry saw a kindred spirit. One who shared the philosophy of helping others and who wasn't afraid to make a stand.

He saw it with his own eyes enough times. He arrived on his sweeping round one day to see Granddad have a coster up against the wall for trying to lift a punnet of strawberries from the display outside the shop.

'If you'd asked me I would have given them to you!' Granddad was shouting.

A few weeks later Henry saw Granddad leading a collection for that same coster.

'We have to look after each other,' Granddad told Henry. 'No one else will.'

'You're right there, George. But there are so many who need help and plenty willing to give it. Some people just need to be asked.'

'I'm not sure about that, Henry. No one round here has much spare as it is. It's like getting blood out of a stone with some people.'

Henry laughed. 'That depends on what you're wearing, George.'

Henry let that hang. Then he said, 'Have you thought of getting involved? Chalton Street could do with its own Pearly King.'

The way Granddad told it, he nearly laughed Henry out of the shop, tea 'n' all. But Henry was persuasive. You have to be if you're going to rattle a collection tin in strangers' faces. Who else knew as many people as George Dole? Who else could spin a yarn like the Dubliner? And who else was already doing his bit to help his fellow costers in their hours of need?

Granddad told me he was never interested but Grandma had a different version.

'The second Henry left he came marching upstairs, yelling, "Emma – have we got any buttons?"'

Somers Town already had its King, but that day the first Pearly King of St Pancras was born.

Granddad wasn't the only local character that Henry was talking to. Up the road in Hampstead there was a young shrimp seller working outside the boozers in Flask Walk. One visit from Henry and suddenly Bert Matthews was anointed the Pearly King of Hampstead. That was three of them, but Henry hadn't finished. He seemed to know so many people that one by one each borough soon had its own 'royal' family. In fact, once word got round what was happening, the movement began to get a life of its own and even people who Henry hadn't met adopted the buttons. Before you knew it, there were twenty-eight Pearly Kings spreading from north to south, one for each borough.

Henry was never an organiser but he did set down one rule. The Pearlies were there to help those less fortunate. They did this by collecting money from entertaining, public appearances or just general tin-rattling. But each Pearly would nominate a charity and that's where every penny would end up. The public needed to be confident in that. The buttons were a badge of honour.

Several places benefited from Henry's generosity. Apart from his orphanage, he also donated to various hospitals, including the London Temperance. This was years before the National Health Service. The poor depended on charity to get basic health care. All the kings had their own causes. Granddad split his collections between the costers themselves and our own local hospital.

Henry and the other kings were only trying to help, not to get noticed. But when you're dressed the way they were and you're making regular donations to this charity or the other, the bush telegraph starts buzzing. In 1907 he was granted an audience with the 'other' royal family when he was introduced to Edward VII and Queen Alexandra at that year's Horse of the Year Show at Olympia. He must have made quite an impression because a few years later one of the highlights of the show was a parade by costermongers leading their donkeys and carts around the show ground. Henry watched from the audience but Granddad, as a true coster himself, was there in his buttons along with Bernie the donkey.

It takes a certain type of person to be a Pearly. You don't just put on the suit – you have to *wear* it. Ask any family of a Pearly King and they'll say the same thing. You transform when you get in the clobber. It doesn't matter what your day job is, when you pull on that suit you are royalty and that's how people treat you. They can't help themselves.

Henry's suit was so completely covered in mother-of-pearl it was more white than black. But he didn't want to make any rules about what other people did. Being a Pearly is all about being a larger-than-life character and so, he thought, that should be reflected in everyone's outfits. That's why you see so many variations today. Each Pearly has his own unique pattern, and, if they give you a twirl, you'll see not only their title spelled out in buttons on their backs like a giant join-the-dots but also a shape or design that's personal to them. Granddad's suit had 'Pearly King of St Pancras' across the shoulders and then underneath that was a large, six-spoked wooden wheel to denote the horse and barrow he used as a coster. Bert's suit had a fish on the back.

We still add that little personal touch today. Look out for a flowerpot if you want to spot a coster. Other people have a cross if they're religious, a horseshoe if they want luck, or an upside-down triangle to denote the ups and downs of life. (Me? I eventually ended up in the merchant navy so I've got a ship on mine. If it means something to you, that makes it more personal than just pulling on a uniform.)

Granddad and the others began to meet up. Because he was close to Hampstead, he and Bert became very good friends. One bonfire night they were going up to the Heath to burn the guy and raise a bit of money for charity. Granddad and Bert both went up in their suits and not only did they raise quite a few quid but Bert walked off with first prize in the fancy dress competition! That was another fiver in the pot for Mount Vernon Hospital.

Although you never stop being a Pearly inside, for everyone else it stops when you hang the suit up at night. Granddad only put his on once a week, usually on a Saturday, when the pubs would be fullest and he could get round a few of them with his collection tin. By then he had nominated the kiddies' hospital in Great Ormond Street for his charity, because he used to walk past it on the way to market. The staff there got used to his regular visits with a box full of coins and even the occasional paper note. He'd get invited in to see the children and, of course, even the visitors in the hospital couldn't help putting their hand in their pocket so he'd have to swing by reception again on his way out with the new loot.

Sometimes he wore the suit at parties if he was invited or if it was a special occasion in the family. Then No. 151 would echo once more with his songs and stories. Those were the nights I really loved.

When she saw how much fun Granddad had, Grandma then joined in as his Pearly Queen. Some of the other families even had Pearly Princes and Princesses but none of my uncles and aunts were interested, not at first. The only person who said 'yes' was Dad. Only once he'd got his suit did one of his sisters pipe up that she fancied being a princess. Of course, it was Annie the twin. Anything her brother could do, so could she.

Annie and Dad made a great couple and with Granddad and Grandma as well they were like a little army of entertainers. Some nights they'd split up for fundraising and other times all four of them would hit the same beer house. I used to beg to go with any of them but kids weren't that popular in pubs so usually the answer was no. But seeing Dad or Aunt Annie do their turns or Granddad and Grandma performing their double act in front of fresh faces was something worth getting told off for. I'd sneak in through the swing doors and hide behind people's legs until I was spotted. Some nights I'd get told off by the landlord, then by Dad for being out, then by Mum for sneaking off without telling her. Three strikes for one bit of naughtiness. But I didn't care. I was hypnotised by the buttons. I couldn't wait to be a grown-up to get a suit of my own.

The only thing that could have made my young life any better was if I'd seen Henry Croft himself. Tragically, according to Granddad, on New Year's Day 1930 Henry was hit by a horse-drawn carriage while collecting outside the Whitechapel Hospital and died later that day in the same workhouse on Charles Street where he had been born sixty-eight years earlier. Some people say he was suffering from cancer at the time. Maybe this was a blessing, going out while he was doing what he liked most. But Granddad was heartbroken. He was losing much more than a friend and Somers Town, he knew, was losing much, much more than a road sweeper – it was losing its unofficial patron saint. He needed to do something, so Granddad went straight to the Croft family and said, 'Leave the arrangements to me.'

Henry was buried at St Pancras cemetery and the funeral, as befits a man who did so much for others, was filmed by Pathé for the news. Granddad had nothing to do with that. You can find a little clip of it online now. And if you do, sadly you can't quite make out Granddad as one of the pallbearers, but you will see a swarm of black-and-white characters; you'll see barrows and donkeys and feathers among the tears because for the funeral of the King of the Pearlies of course every 'royal' family in London turned up. By 1930 there were about 400 including Queens and Princes and Princesses, who all owed their way of lives to one man.

Of course, Henry touched a lot more people than just us, which is why his cortege stretched back more than half a mile down the street. Thousands of costers and market traders gave up their day's work to come along (although plenty sold a bit of fruit along the way), and then there were all the 'ordinary' people who just wanted to pay their respects to a man who stood out for all the good he did. A lot of the people he helped turned up as well and some of the charities he sponsored clubbed together to pay for a statue of Henry in his buttons to stand over the grave.

During the funeral speech, it was announced that Henry had

raised more than five grand for various charities. In today's money we're talking nigh on a quarter of a million! And that's all without social media or adverts or getting help from celebrities. It was all done the old-fashioned way of walking up to strangers and encouraging them to dig deep.

When Granddad used to describe the day, and the way Henry was carried through the streets of north London on a carriage pulled by two black horses with black-and-white plumes, I wished and wished I'd been there. Then one day I actually said it and Granddad laughed.

'But you were there!'

I accused him of telling porkie pies, of course, because I knew he'd died weeks before I'd been born. But I was surprised to hear Dad backed up his story. Of course, Granddad and Grandma and Dad had ridden along in their cart, pulled by Tommy the horse, at pride of place at the front of the procession. But they weren't the only ones. Mum never got involved in Pearly business, aside from helping with the sewing, but she knew what it meant to the family so she went along as well – even in her condition. I might just have been an unborn baby in my mother's belly but to this day, I am proud to say I was there, witnessing Henry Croft, the founder of the Pearlies, going to his Maker. It meant a lot to me later to learn that I was there. People laugh when I say I feel a connection with Henry. But I was there, at his funeral, before I'd even been born. That's not a coincidence. I reckon he's inside every one of us Pearlies. Cut us in half and I reckon Henry'll step out!

Of course, I didn't believe that back then. My years of being a Pearly King were years away. Right then I was content to enjoy the life through Granddad and Dad's eyes. After all, as a six-year-old I had plenty of other important things on my mind.

Like having fun.

4

Us Against the World

Being around Granddad and the Pearly Kings was an enjoyable part of my life. But it wasn't all of it, not by a long chalk. The memories of those nights just stand out more as I look back now. The truth is, I had enough on my plate without the business of buttons.

Although Mum gave up her Romany way of life when she met my dad, certain habits died hard. Just because we weren't on wheels, it didn't mean we couldn't get around. By the time I was sixteen we'd moved house a dozen times. There wasn't a street between Euston and Somers Town where my dad hadn't laid his hat. From Bridgeway we went to Cranleigh Street, then Medburn, Northdown, Royal College, Aldenham, Charrington, back to Medburn, and so on and so on. We were constantly on the go, upping sticks once every six months sometimes. We moved so often that when Rags got off his lead one day, he ran back to the place we'd lived in two houses ago. He wasn't the only one. Dad came home one night steaming drunk and was met by a confused-looking woman in the kitchen who said, 'Alfie, you don't live here any more.'

Because everyone just left their keys on bits of string inside the letterbox, or had the latch itself wired up to a bit of thread you'd just tug, he'd just let himself in as normal.

We weren't the only people who moved around a lot. I heard of a lot of families who did a moonlight flit when their rent was due. They were there when I went to bed then gone by breakfast. But we always moved in daytime, as far as I remember, so I don't think we could have been running away from anyone. In any case, sometimes we only went a hundred yards down the street – not the best place to hide from the landlord.

Sometimes we moved to a cheaper place when work was thin on the ground but then when Dad could afford it we'd upgrade again. Usually it was for the extra space. When we were in Bridgeway Street I shared a room with David. When we moved on, Mum had had another baby, my little sister Rosie, so we needed an extra room. By the time I was six she'd also had Marjorie and was pregnant again, with my brother Wally on the way. Sleeping two or three to a bed wasn't uncommon, depending on where we lived. In the winter it kept us warm, especially with no heating upstairs. And it was better than a wooden box.

Apart from the amount of rooms, most of the places were the same. Brown or flowered wallpaper, outdoor lavatories and a front room that Mum kept under lock and key. All that really changed was the amount of people. Sometimes we had a flat so there'd be other families upstairs. Sometimes we had a little narrow terraced house and it would be just us. Sometimes we'd have a whole house and rent out a room or two to relatives. Bill and Polly spent a lot of time with us.

But it didn't matter where we ended up, I still played the same games with the same kids on the same streets. They were our playgrounds. Apart from the occasional horse and cart and an irate coster chasing some scally over the cobbles you pretty much had the roads to yourselves. No one in Somers Town had a car. One or two, like Granddad, had access to a lorry for work but that was it. You had to go to one of the busier link roads to see a real-life motor, bombing along Eversholt Street, or Hampstead or Euston Road. Even then they were outnumbered five to one by the new trolley buses with their distinctive curved rears and adverts plastered all over the side.

Although we were lucky to be so space-rich, we'd have been luckier to have a few toys or bicycles to play with. But everyone was as borassic (*boracic lint*, *skint*) as everyone else. But that was all right. We were kids. We had imaginations that would power a steam train.

Cricket was the big game in summer. At least our version of it was. One of the kids had a small rubber ball, so we'd bowl that down Bridgeway Street, or wherever we were living, and the kid the other end would try to whack it with an old chair leg or a crate slat or whatever piece of wood we'd managed to scramble. Wickets would be old Jaffa crates I'd scrounge from No. 151. Very versatile, those old things.

None of us knew the rules of the game – the closest I got to seeing a real match was standing on Dad's shoulders trying to peep into Lord's when he took me down to St John's Wood – but we all knew how to chase a ball. Some days there were thirty-odd urchins haring after it like dogs after a fox and by the time one of us got it there was no one left to throw it to!

There was a variation on the cricket which was also a laugh – if you were quick enough. I think it's a bit more like baseball, really, because instead of getting the batsman out by hitting the stumps when he's running, you could just throw the ball at him instead. You needed to be lively to play that – and have a head made of rock.

That would go on and on all day, until we either smashed something or it all descended into a giant fight because someone didn't like being bowled in the wotsits. Then we'd all get called in for our tea and it would be forgotten.

Sometimes, after I'd eaten, I'd go back out to see who was about. If none of the other kids were allowed back, I'd just race Rags up and down. I'd give myself a head start then throw a stick and see who could get it first.

You have energy to burn as kids, don't you? Sometimes if we couldn't find a ball (or if a dog ran off with it) we'd play football with a tin can. That was the cricket story all over again. Every kid would follow the 'ball', like a swarm of bees, and if you did get hold of it there'd be no one to pass to and no one in goal.

If someone was lucky enough to get a whip and top, we'd spend days on end playing it, usually not even stopping to eat. The harder you whack the top, the faster it spins. It's simple but it keeps your attention.

Real toys like that, though, were few and far between so we

had to improvise. Anything that wasn't tied down became a potential plaything for me. I'd have fun spinning bottles, throwing stones at old spam tins or, when Granddad wasn't looking, seeing how big an explosion I could get out of lobbing a rancid orange at his side wall.

I remember once finding some rope in Granddad's yard. It was near his horse gear but, as I reasoned to myself, he wasn't using it at that moment so that made it 'free'. Even as I left the yard I wasn't sure what to do with it, but then inspiration struck. Two mates gave me a leg up a lamppost, then they threw the rope up and I tied it to the top. For the rest of the day we took it in turns to hang onto the loose end and swing ourselves round until we got too dizzy or scraped our knees too much to walk. It was a roundabout, a swing and a maypole dance all in one, and it all started with that piece of 'borrowed' rope.

You took your fun where you could. Tibby Cat, Tin Copper Charlie, Leapfrog, Hopscotch – none of them needed anything other than a bit of chalk or a stick of wood and dozens of you could play at once.

Those were all the games we played when we were being good little children just trying to keep out of the adults' hair. It usually wasn't very long before someone suggested Knock Down Ginger and then the stakes were raised. Daring each other to knock on so-and-so's door and run away before she opened it seemed like the naughtiest thing in the world. You couldn't say no because you'd be called a coward or – worse – a girl, so you had to go through with it. There was another version we played called Knock Dolly Out Of Bed. You could only do this with a bit of string. We'd tie it to a door knocker then hide round the corner, tug the string and listen for the woman of the house to answer the door. Normally they didn't notice the string until the third or fourth time, then the air could turn blue. We'd be off like scalded cats while she was still screaming what she was going to do to us.

With Ginger or Dolly you got extra points if you knew a bloke was in because he would chase you if he saw you – and you'd get a whack if you were too slow. That's if you were lucky. The worst thing was being dragged by the ear or the scruff of the neck back to your house, because your own mum and dad would do worse.

The wrath of your elders was one of those things you had to put up with. Granddad had a large black belt that he threatened me with from time to time – like, for example, when he discovered I'd left his best cart rope tied to a lamppost and it had got nicked. He was furious. He yanked the belt out of his buckles and held it above his head like he was going to whip his horses. I burst into tears, swearing that I would get it back, that I'd never go in his yard again, and other promises I had no chance of keeping. He just shook his head and left the room.

Like everything with Granddad, it was a bit theatrical. But that didn't stop me nearly wetting myself with fear. Grandma was lovely. She never contradicted Granddad in front of him, but as soon as he disappeared she gave me a cloth to wipe my tears and then, as I left the shop, slipped me an apple.

'Our little secret,' she said with a wink.

I was too terrified to go back into No. 151 for days. When I did pluck up the courage Granddad couldn't have been happier to see me. Not only did he not mention how I'd let him down, he had a surprise for me.

A length of rope.

'Just ask next time, Alfred, will you?'

It wasn't my last run-in with my grandfather or the last time I was threatened with the belt. But he never once laid hand or leather on me. It was just for show.

Dad was much the same. Some of my mates could get a wallop if they spilled their milk at teatime. Dad was never like that. He was a gentle man, not one to raise his hands at all if he could help it. When things kicked off in the beer houses, he was the one to try to placate both sides. But he had his limits. And if you pushed him, you would know all about it.

The easiest way to push him was to pick on his woman. 'You may as well unleash the dogs of war,' my grandma, Emma, said. I asked her what she meant and she told me about a time when Dad and Mum were still courting. As I've said, Dad would walk to the East End to save money so he and his girlfriend could afford a bus when they went out. They caught a bus one night and because it was a busy Saturday night it was standing room only. While Dad looked around for a seat for his Mary, a bloke with a funny accent called out to her. Dad let it go the first time, but when another guy with the same accent said something cheeky he stepped over. It turned out there were seven of them, all sailors from Norway, looking for a good night out after disembarking at the West India Docks. By the state of them, the party had already started.

'Listen,' Dad said to all of them, 'in this country we don't talk about a girl like that.'

There was silence on the bus. Everyone had heard him. And everyone knew from the tone of his voice that he meant business. Everyone English, that is.

Maybe it lost something in translation.

Dad had turned back to be with Mum when one of the sailors said something else about her figure. That was it. The guy was still laughing when Dad smacked him in the mouth. Then, before his mates could get up, he punched them all as well. It helped they were all trapped in by the tight rows of seats. It also helped that they were two sheets gone. But, Grandma reckons, they wouldn't have stopped Dad if there'd been twenty of them.

It was over within a minute. Then when the bus stopped next Dad said, 'This is your stop, lads,' before grabbing the first sailor and dragging him off. The others didn't budge so Dad cracked one of them again. They high-tailed it soon enough then.

Over the years I saw Dad walk away from more fights than he had. He was a man of principle and he couldn't stand seeing anyone waving a weapon around. A lot of young guys liked to carry a 'chiv' – one of the old open razors. Dad said he'd personally sort me out if he ever caught me with one.

'If you can't have a straight fight then don't bother.'

I only saw the harder side of my father a couple of times but that was enough. I didn't think I deserved it at the time but looking back, of course I did! For example, when I decided to win myself a prize.

The little shop opposite our house – we were in Charrington Street by then – sold meat, cheese and tinned goods, but it also had a range of tall jars packed with exotic things like gobstoppers and black jacks. You could get a bagful for a penny, and once in a blue moon a penny would find its way into my little palm so I'd head straight over.

Sweets weren't the only thing you could get for a penny in that shop. There was a kind of fruit machine for kids there which, if you got lucky, would pay out in little toys. Given the choice, I'd always spend my penny on sweets. But the dream was to have two pence and have both.

That never looked likely to happen, not when I was five, not when I was six, and not when I was seven. Then one day I saw Dad sorting through a box on his bed. I didn't have to go in the room to know what was making that rattling noise in the box. It was money.

A plan was forming.

I got away with it once. Then once more. My mistake was going back again and again. Eventually, of course, Dad noticed his box of coins was a lot lighter. If they'd all disappeared he'd have thought he'd been burgled. The fact just a handful were missing told him someone was trying to be clever.

'Alfred!'

He used my real name. That's when I knew I was in trouble.

I knew we were poor but I honestly could not see why Dad was so furious. He was shouting at me all sorts about what would happen if I didn't return his coins.

But he never said 'pennies'.

I learned later that these were no ordinary coins. Dad had been working with a demolition crew for the last few months and he'd taken down a church. All the gold and metals had been stripped long before the first sledgehammer blow. As the church came down even the wood, stones and lead roof were being half-inched. But only Dad kept on smashing, so he was the one who found the little earthenware pot buried in the foundations. The pot had some words in foreign – Latin probably – on the side but it was the contents that caught his eye: coins. A handful, buried to ask God for good luck when the church was constructed.

Dad had never seen the like before but he had the wit to hide them from his workmates.

Unfortunately, he didn't hide them well enough from me.

I could only plead ignorance for so long. Then I had to confess that his precious coins were inside the slot machine across the road.

'Come with me!'

He dragged me over to the shop and explained the situation to Mr Owen the shopkeeper. Unfortunately, Owen also had an idea what the coins were worth.

'Listen,' Dad said, desperately trying to keep his cool, 'if you don't give me my coins I'll get the police on you.'

'Good luck with that, Alf Dole. I'll tell them your son has been fiddling my machine with fake pennies! It'll be borstal for him.'

The last thing Dad really wanted to do was involve the law. But he knew the guy was right. I had voluntarily put the coins in. No one had made me. And, as much as Dad wanted to snap the shopkeeper's thieving neck, it went against his own code. Tail between his legs, he left the shop, dragging me with him.

I'd had the worst of it before we went over the road. Dad looked broken. He sent me to my room and went out to the pub –

taking his near-empty box with him. The worst thing was, I'd wasted all his money and never won a single prize on the machine.

A few weeks later the shop opposite changed hands. Some people said the old owner had come into money and moved on. But others said he'd been threatened to walk away while he could.

If I'm making my dad out to be some sort of saint, he wasn't. He wasn't a bad 'un by any stretch but he knew how to let his hair down. 'Mad Alf', his brothers and sisters would call him, because they never knew what he was going to do next – and because he could never back down from a dare.

He was out one night with a couple of his brothers. Night was actually turning into the early hours of the morning and, as they passed Euston Station, the hotels around there were busy with their laundry. One of them had four large wicker baskets packed with dirty towels and linen lined up outside.

'Bet you couldn't lift one of those, Alf,' Bill said.

'You're joking, aren't you? I could carry one home.'

'Dare you.'

Bill had said the magic words.

'You're on,' Dad said, so over he ran and, while his brothers kept watch, somehow managed to lift this huge basket over his head. Then he was off, running up Eversholt Street.

The next morning he woke up with a sore head – and twenty-two towels and fifteen sheets piled up on top of him. Through the haze of his hangover he could make out the raven-haired shape of his wife standing over him.

'What the hell have you been up to now, Alfie Dole?'

Then she laughed, left the room – and sent me and Rags up to jump on him.

Even though we'd ended up with a lifetime's supply of linen, Dad didn't see it as pinching. To him it was just a bit of fun. If he'd had his way, he'd have returned the lot as soon as his head cleared. But Mum wouldn't hear of it. That's why she was laughing. She was happy he'd carried the basket home, even if it did mean a week's worth of laundry for her (and remember, it was all done by hand then wrung out by a mangle kept in the yard). But then Mum had a different view of shopping to most people.

I don't meant to be insulting when I say it's a gypsy thing – because that's what she called it – but the truth was, Mum saw nothing wrong with being a bit light-fingered. There were two kinds of shopping as far as she was concerned. The stuff she paid for, and the things she didn't.

Shops like Granddad's and the sweet shop were off limits to Mum. Partly because they sold everything across the counter and partly because they were run by ordinary people earning a crust. But the big department stores that were opening up, like Debenhams on Oxford Street, they were ripe for the picking.

It started for me one day when I wasn't allowed out to play. Mum was pregnant with my brother Wally, so she said, 'I'm popping to the shops. You can come and carry my bags.'

She called them 'bags' but even carried by her they nearly came down to the ground. The only way I could stop them dragging on the floor was to sling them over my shoulder like Father Christmas. And the weight! She'd made them herself by cutting up an old sofa and stitching the leather together – so, not only were they tough, they were also pretty heavy when they were empty. And they wouldn't be empty for long.

Whatever Mum hoped to buy, there was going to be a lot of it. What I didn't realise that first time was that 'buying' was the last thing on her mind. As we walked around Debenhams, she passed me a jumper here, a skirt there, a pair of shoes from the other aisle and even a jacket.

'Squeeze it in, Boy-Boy,' she ordered me. 'I don't want to see anything sticking out.'

I still hadn't twigged. Other people were carrying baskets. We had bags. What was the difference?

That became clear a few minutes later when Mum decided to leave.

'But we haven't paid, Mum?'

'Just keep walking,' she said, 'and lift those bags up!'

She was a nightmare, she really was. But, I have to be honest, I got a thrill out of helping her. For a young kid, it was just fun – naughty fun. And, the thing is, you don't think to question your parents at that age. You probably never do, if I'm honest.

Mum didn't need me when she wasn't pregnant – not that she looked any different by the end of it. Dad wasn't the only one who could use a needle and thread. With a little cutting and stitching she turned an ordinary winter coat into her special 'shopping' number. Inside it had pockets in the lining the size of carrier bags. If she could get something in the opening, she could carry it hands-free. Even if she had the coat open, you couldn't see the booty squirrelled away inside. After a morning's shopping it wasn't unusual for her to come home looking eight months gone. Anyone who saw her go into the shop would be left scratching their heads.

Like Dad with his fists, Mum had her moral code. Dad could leave his Pearly collections around the house without being worried they'd disappear before he delivered them to Great Ormond Street. They didn't even need to discuss it. Mum only took from the faceless organisations she knew could afford it. She didn't judge what Dad did, and he didn't judge her.

'Never forget,' they both used to tell me, 'it's us against the world.'

I liked that rule, even as a kid. It meant the same as the other saying they had: 'Blood is thicker than water'. Just like costers looked out for each other, you never, ever, go against the family. That was a code I could live by.

I just wish other members of my family had been able to live by it as well.

5

Will Someone Give
Me A Guinea?

Door keys on bits of string. Borrowing a cup of sugar from your neighbours. Looking after your own. It sounds like a storybook version of London in the 'old days' but that's really how we lived, more or less. And a lot of those ways, you'd have to agree, we could do with bringing back today.

Not all of them, mind.

On the nights when Dad wasn't out Pearlying he'd sometimes take Mum out for a stout and blackcurrant. They'd always done this, even when I was a baby. It never occurred to me until later to ask who'd looked after me while they were out.

'Oh, you were all right. Rags was there.'

Now, I loved Rags with all my young heart. But trusting him to babysit? Maybe it wasn't quite such a fairy tale after all back then.

We were poor. I was in no doubt about that. Dad would be

paid on a Friday, which meant Saturday was 'meat' day when we'd eat well. Gradually as the week went on, the meals got greyer and more soupy. By Thursday we'd be on carrot broth – luckily we had no shortage of those. Pudding, occasionally, might be a cake if Mum had time and eggs to bake. More often I'd have a slice of bread with sugar spread on it if we could spare any.

But, food aside, the advantage of having sixteen aunts and uncles (and their spouses – Uncle Patsy excepted) is that an abundant supply of hand-me-downs was constantly arriving. Sometimes I'd be lucky and the clothes and bits and pieces would be 'as new'. Other times I might be the twentieth Dole grand-child to receive them. It's bad enough when we're talking about bonnets and booties. But I also know for a fact nappies were passed around the family as well. It doesn't bear thinking about.

It wasn't just the grown-ups who swapped things around. I was into recycling years before the council gave us a blue bin. To be honest, though, I wasn't thinking about the environment.

One of the big jam manufacturers used to reuse its jam jars whenever it could get its hands on them. The way they did this was to offer a price on each jar. For most people it wasn't worth the effort of sending back but if you collected enough it could be worth your while. One bloke made it his business to grab as many as he could. He'd drive around the streets with a horse and cart, and on the back, next to a small skip for the jars, was a little merry-go-round suspended from an arm on a pivot. He'd call out to all the kids, 'Bring us your jam jars and you can have a ride.'

It was the highlight of the week when he came round. He used to ring a bell like the old totters (rag 'n' bone men) so you knew he was coming. I'd fly into the house and grab any empties we'd put aside. Then I'd tear out and queue up with the other lucky beggars. It wasn't exactly the roller coaster at Alton Towers — when you got on the swing, he'd crank a handle and you'd have two minutes spinning around on a little chair — but it was a damn sight better than grazing your hands swinging round a lamppost on a stolen rope. With no playgrounds in the borough, it was the only time we got to go on anything like it.

I was always pestering Mum and Grandma to let me have a jam jar because of him. Sometimes I'd beg for jam and bread for my pudding just so we'd use it up sooner. More than once when we heard that bell I persuaded Mum to scoop the jam into a bowl just so I could get a spin. She'd moan, of course, but she always did it.

Glass must have been in short supply because the manufacturers of lemonade and other soft drinks ran similar schemes. Sadly, no one sent a funfair round, but if you took a bottle back to one of the pubs or Mr White's grocer's shop, they'd give you a penny. That only worked if you drank lemonade, which we didn't because it was too expensive. But that didn't stop me combing the bins for throwaways or hanging around Mr White's in case someone dropped an empty on the way out.

Occasionally I went even further. Roaming the streets with Rags after dark one day — it was only about five o'clock, but it was winter — I noticed the gate open round the back of the Red Lion. There by the back door was a crate of lemonade empties ready to be sent back.

How could I resist that? I was only my mother's son, after all.

I wished I'd had one of her bags! I could comfortably hold four bottles, so of course I went for a fifth — and dropped it. It didn't smash but it did bounce and hit the concrete three or four times, each bounce echoing around the still yard.

Time to go!

I was out of sight before anyone arrived at the back door. But I was still close enough to hear a barmaid say, 'How did you get in, Rags?' then heard her shut the gate. I spent the whole night hoping she never put two and two together.

However good the system of swaps and hand-me-downs, there was one thing we were always short of. When I started school Mum said, 'You'll only be going every other day.'

That sounded good to me. But I had to ask, 'Why's that, Mum?'

'Because we've only got one pair of boots — and David'll be wearing them the rest of the time.'

It seems crazy now. Why didn't I go in my 'day shoes'? But uniforms are uniforms, and we had just half of one.

Anyway, it gave me more time to play out with whoever else hadn't made it in to class. Usually it was Rags. Life was good.

Then, when I was nearly seven, my world caved in. Rags got ill. I didn't know what was wrong with him and neither did anyone else. We couldn't afford to take him to a vet. Night after night he lay with me at the end of my bed as usual, always finding my feet and not Rosie's, and every morning I'd expect to be woken up by him licking my face. Every morning he was still where I'd left him. If I hadn't carried him down to eat I don't think he would have bothered. His bladder started letting him down as well, even though he wasn't drinking anything. When I went to school I took him over to Granddad's yard rather than worry what mess he'd make in the house with me away.

It was a good plan, I thought. Nothing could go wrong.

When I came home that afternoon I went straight to the yard's Cranleigh Street entrance. I called Rags' name but I wasn't surprised when he didn't answer. He'd been like that for a few days. When I went in, though, he wasn't where I'd left him.

Fantastic, I thought, *he's up and about*.

I went dashing into the shop, happy as you like, and found Granddad talking to my Uncle Mike.

'Have you seen Rags?' I asked them. 'He must be better because he's escaped from the yard.'

Granddad didn't answer. Instead he looked at his son.

'It's for the best,' Uncle Mike said.

'What is?' I asked.

'The mutt was in so much pain I put him out of his misery.'

'You did what?'

'I drowned him. He's better off now.'

At first I thought he was joking. He had to be. Then I looked at Granddad who, for once, was lost for words.

I think I might have sworn because as I barged past them and out of the shop I remember Uncle Mike yelling angrily at me to come back. But I didn't stop running until I got home. When I told Mum her mouth fell open in disbelief. She grabbed my collar and dragged me back round to No. 151. Uncle Mike was still there – and more fool him for that. Because whatever I'd said in rage, Mum screamed ten times worse. Uncle Mike refused to back down, saying he'd done it for us because he knew we were too poor to pay for treatment.

'I was doing you a favour, you silly cow!'

It was at that point Granddad had to shut the shop. Mum might have been tiny but she was no pushover. For a minute I thought she was actually going to hit her brother-in-law.

'If Alfie were here he would lamp you!' she screamed.

'Of course he wouldn't. He's not as sentimental as you.'

And that's when she did hit him.

When Dad came home from work I started telling him what his brother had done. Before I could finish, Mum interrupted.

'I'll do this,' she said.

Dad sat quietly until she'd finished. By the end he was so still I thought he was just going to shrug it off.

'I don't know why you're making all this fuss,' I expected him to say.

But he didn't. He said, 'Leave Mikey to me,' and he left the house. When he returned hours later I was in bed, unable to sleep. I kept thinking about Rags. He should have been on my feet, circling and circling until he got comfy, pulling up the covers in the process until Rosie shouted at him to lay still. But he wasn't there. I pictured his face in that barrel. I pictured his big brown eyes looking up at Uncle Mike through the water and I felt sick. Who could do that to an animal? Who could do that to my Rags?

I must have dropped off eventually because when I woke the next day I got up as normal and went downstairs. When I got to the kitchen and saw the little tin bowl on the floor it all came flooding back. I couldn't go to school that day. Or the next. I spent every spare hour I had walking the streets where I used to run with Rags alongside me. Some adults said I'd get over it. I hated them for that. Why would I want to?

For three months after that we didn't see Mike or his wife or his kids. They didn't come to Granddad's, they weren't around for Pearly nights, and with Christmas fast approaching, no one was expecting them to put in an appearance. They weren't the only ones who were threatening not to show. The whole family was split. Half the Doles were on Mike's side; the rest were with us. Yes, we're a close family, but you don't go around drowning someone else's dog.

The closer we got to Christmas Day the more guilty I began to feel. Rags had been ill and, yes, maybe he was in a better place now. Had I done the right thing making such a fuss? Maybe I needed to apologise. Mum wouldn't hear of anything of the sort.

'It's that silly-arse uncle of yours who's caused all this,' she said. 'If anyone's going to say sorry, it's him.'

I didn't hold out much hope but Christmas does funny things to people. We went round to Granddad's as usual and there among all the people on 'our' side were the others. Most of them, anyway. Only one family was missing: Mike's.

But then Dad came over and said there was someone who wanted to see me. I followed him downstairs and there was Uncle Mike. He looked as awkward as I felt. I was a kid. I wasn't used to people apologising to me, so I just stared at the floor and mumbled, 'It's okay,' when he'd finished. But as far as I was concerned it was over. Rags had gone but I wanted my family – all my family – back together again. Especially on that day of all days.

As for any celebration, No. 151 was the place to be at Christmas. This year Granddad really pulled the stops out. Instead of decorations he hung all his unsold fruit from the ceiling. Everywhere you looked there were bananas and grapes and oranges and pears. Then, at the end of the day, we were all allowed to grab a piece. I don't think anyone noticed, let alone cared, that it had all been hidden by a cloud of smoke for the whole day. It was the only present most of us were likely to receive so we were grateful. We all knew how tight Granddad was with his fruit.

It made me so sad to fall out with my relatives (or at least be the cause of friction between them) because so many of them were always there for me. Sometimes 'there' was more like 'here'.

When we moved to Northdown Street, we shared the house with Uncle Bill and Aunt Polly. It was a big old place; so big that me and David had our own little rooms, with Wally, Marjorie and Rosie together in another. Rosie got to play 'mum' with the young 'uns, whether she liked it or not. It was nice to have a bit of space but it was even nicer to know your family was just the other side of a door – literally, on one occasion.

While Aunt Polly was a diamond, having Uncle Bill around gave me sleepless nights. He loved to tell me there were ghosts and that he could spot them. I was terrified but fascinated at the same time. One night just after Christmas, when it had been dark since about three in the afternoon, he called me over.

'Look out there,' he said, pointing in the blackness. 'Can you see it?'

'See what?' I said. 'It's too dark.'

'Behind the tree. Can you see it?'

I screwed my eyes up and pressed my nose against the window. I knew there was a big old maple on the pavement outside but I was beggared if I could make it out.

'What's there?' I asked.

'Do you really want to know?'

I nodded, although I really wasn't that sure.

'It's a ghost.'

I knew it! I felt a shiver up my spine just at the thought.

'You don't believe me, do you?' Uncle Bill said. 'Well, go out and see for yourself if you want.'

I was worried he was going to say that. I was already terrified but at six years old, nearly seven, the most powerful emotion I had was curiosity. That trumped a silly old thing like fear.

'Okay,' I said. 'I'll go.'

I went to the front door and didn't look back. For some reason it seemed important to me that Uncle Bill didn't see me scared. I opened the door and ran out. The second I did I heard a slam. The door had shut. When I looked at the front window, there was Uncle Bill – laughing his head off.

Sod the ghost, I just wanted to get back in.

I tried the handle but it was locked. Fine. I stuck my hand through the letterbox and tried to grab the key. The string should have been right there but I couldn't find it. When I looked again at the window, I saw Uncle Bill was holding the key, string and all.

Gone went my desire not to seem afraid. I burst into tears and started banging on the door. Ghost or not, I did not want to be out there one second longer.

When the door was flung open, it was Aunt Polly standing there. At that moment I honestly felt she'd saved my life. Before long she would do it for real.

I remember Mum and Dad going out one night. Rags wasn't around to look after me and the others and Bill had gone out as well, so that left Aunt Polly. She put us to bed about nine and then I heard her go up herself half an hour later. That gave me the chance to do what I'd been dreaming of for months. I crept downstairs and went into the kitchen and immediately saw what I was looking for. The fire was still crackling from earlier – the heat from that hearth was our central heating in those days. I checked the door again for sight or sound of Aunt Polly then reached into my pyjama pocket. It was there. The thing I'd had stashed for a week. The thing I'd 'borrowed' from No. 151 at the last party.

A cigarette.

It had fallen out from behind someone's ear and I was closest to the ground so I'd found it. Now it was mine.

I knew what to do. I'd seen Mum and Dad do it enough times. I held it near the closest flame and waited a second. Even though it was made of paper, it didn't flare up like I feared. After a few seconds I pulled it away and looked at the end. It was glowing. Perfect. As quickly as I could I ran back up to my room.

Of course, I thought I knew it all, but I had a lot to learn. By the time I was back in my bed, the glow had disappeared. I gave it a couple of sucks and that just made me cough, but nothing else seemed to be happening.

I must be doing something wrong, I decided. *Ah well, it tasted disgusting anyway.*

So I took it out of my mouth, rolled over and fell asleep.

The next thing I knew, Aunt Polly was shouting at me to get up. When I opened my eyes I saw her jumping up and down on the floor. Then I realised she was jumping on my blankets.

And they were on fire.

On the long list of things I didn't know about cigarettes, not realising when they were alight or not was top of the list. Fortunately for me, more smoke had gone under my door and along the hallway to my aunt's room than in my lungs. Even more luckily, she hadn't been asleep.

Not only did she manage to get the fire out, she also changed my bed and promised she wouldn't tell Mum – but only if I swore never to try smoking again.

She didn't need to ask me twice.

A new year meant another birthday and it turned out to be a landmark one. Now I was seven, Mum announced, I needed to be doing more around the house – although it turned out to be anywhere but.

When she wasn't having babies or carrying them – there was now Dave, me, Rosie, Marje and Wally – she ran a Sunday market stall up in Camden Town, just far enough away so as not to queer Granddad's pitch. It was already a family operation even without me and, because Dad already had a job, it started at the weekend. On Saturdays he went down to the sidings at York Way, where the trains emptied their loads. Then he and all the wholesalers from Covent Garden would grab what they needed. Compared to the others, Dad's needs were few. Beetroot was his thing, so he'd grab a couple of hundredweight of that and whatever else was fresh, like mint, celery, anything for a salad.

Anyone could sell a beetroot but Mum's were different. They were cooked. When Dad got home I helped him unload them all into the big copper – a giant cooking pot – and I gave them all a wash. Then he put the copper over the fire and boiled the lot. While that was going on I washed the celery and leaves in the kitchen sink then patted it all down with a towel. Mum chopped it all up and, when the beetroot was ready, she bagged it all.

She didn't have a barrow and she didn't have a shop – but she did have a way of asking people for favours that they couldn't refuse. While all the hawkers and costers got wet in the elements, she made her patch under the canopy up at the greengrocer's where Sainsbury's supermarket is now. Like No. 151 they weren't allowed to open on a Sunday, so not only did Mum keep dry, she ensured customers knew they could always get fruit and veg at that location seven days a week.

The shop might have been closed but there were plenty of competitors around. But Mum did all right. When she put her mind to it she could charm the birds from the trees with all her patter. She was like Dad and Granddad in that way, a natural. That didn't stop her trading, though. Anything she had left at the end of the day was used to barter with another seller. Sunday nights were feasts. Grapes, seafood, apples. We could get a lot of it from Granddad but self-sufficiency was our way. That was the lesson.

Helping out at home was one thing. Granddad, though, offered me the chance to earn my first wage.

'But,' he said, 'you'll have to earn it!'

He was right about that. Four o'clock on Monday morning he was already outside his stables on Camley Mews. He had a tall, brown cob called Tommy, the one who had pulled his cart at Henry Croft's funeral and taken part in Horse of the Year parades, but Tom wasn't the one pulling Granddad's barrow today. That was Granddad himself. Why? I had no idea. I'd walked down to Covent Garden and further but never with a barrow. We were barely over the Euston Road when I said, 'Can I have a ride?'

'What do you think this is? A funfair?'

Still, even as he spoke, Granddad slowed the cart so I could clamber over the wheels and on board.

'You're lucky it's all downhill,' he grumbled. 'On the way back you can push me.'

So on we went, through the streets of London. The *quiet* streets of London. I thought the city never slept. Yet here it was, almost snoring. The only noise I could hear was the crunch of the wooden wheels against the cobbled stones. On a normal day on Chalton Street you wouldn't even notice it. That morning it sounded like we were bringing thunder to Kingsway.

Gradually, though, it started to pick up as we joined another barrow at one junction, then two more at the next. By the time we were within sight of Covent Garden I could see at least a hundred others like us – although Granddad's barrow was the only one with a passenger. By the time we reached the giant stone pillars at the entrance there must have been a thousand. And the noise!

This was what London should sound like.

No one spoke, though. They shouted. Shouted hello, shouted their orders, shouted where so-and-so could stick his prices. Everything was at top volume. And yet above all that din I could make out the same sound over and over.

'Morning, Specky!'

Men I couldn't even see were calling it out and Granddad was hollering back their names in return. I'd never seen him called 'Specky' before. It was like he had a completely different life in the market.

We loaded the barrow with the best bargains he could find. My job was packing everything neatly so it wouldn't fall off when we got going, then guarding the purchases while Granddad wandered around looking for more. Condemned oranges were a bit scarce but he found a few and I heaved them onto the cart while he moved on to the next stall. When he was satisfied, we dragged the load over to the main exit and started pushing back the way we'd come. It was six o'clock by now. People were out and about on the streets. I never thought I'd be in a traffic jam at that ungodly hour but at times we were. As we came to the end of Great Queen Street, Granddad decided to have a rest against a tram stop. The trams in those days ran north to south along Southampton Row. Or at least, I thought he was resting.

'I'll see you at home, Alfie,' he announced. 'I'm taking the tram home.'

'What?'

'It's only fair – I pushed here. Now you push back.'

'But, but . . . it's uphill. And . . .' I lifted the barrow handles and gave a shove. ' . . . I can't budge it on my own.'

'Well you'll just have to try harder. Here comes my tram.'

I turned away and tried to shove the barrow again. This time it moved a few inches but I couldn't see it going much further. The fruit was going to be rotten before I got it home.

Then a hand slapped me on the back. It was Granddad. He'd only been winding me up – I think.

For my trouble he gave me two shillings. That became my regular job. On school days I was back in time and on David's turn for the shoes, I went to bed. I'd earned it, actually earned it. It felt good.

Having Tommy and a cart but pushing a barrow to market instead seemed madness to me. But Tommy was a heavy-goods puller, Granddad said. It wasn't worth the effort getting him all harnessed up when he could shove the barrow himself. Still, when he said he was going to buy a new horse I assumed all that was going to change, especially when he said he was looking to buy a donkey – the original costermonger mode of transport. When he asked if I'd like to earn some more pocket money by coming with him, I leaped at it. Even though it was my turn to go to school, I didn't think anyone would mind, or even notice.

Our destination was the horse auction across the river at Elephant and Castle. The London Repository, as it was called, used to stand exactly where the Charlie Chaplin pub is now, on the south side of the street at number 16–18 New Kent Road. I don't mind a swift half in the Chaplin these days but, I have to say, the old building on its site was a lot more fun for a seven-year-old. In fact, the fun began on our journey there. Going on trams for me was a rare luxury, especially with the round-backed trolley buses beginning to take over more space on the main roads, so the chance to get one of the old electric carts made the day worthwhile from the start. Granddad paid the conductor and we stood looking out at the passing costers, barrowboys and shopkeepers setting up for the day. Compared to the barrow it was a lot quieter once it got going but it was a bit jerky with it.

The Repository was essentially a wall with a load of stables and garages the other side, because it was also used to shift the new motor cars as well. On the morning we were there – and it was morning, another six o'clock job if you don't mind – it was just old-fashioned horsepower on sale.

The place was already fairly busy with dozens of men in the same uniform of the time – dark overcoats, brown or black trousers, a waistcoat and shirt and, of course, a cap or trilby hat to set it off – all studying the printed catalogue then going over to the stables to size up the respective lot. Granddad fitted right in. He was dressed the same and like everyone else he only had eyes for the horses and their write-ups. Getting a bargain was the number-one priority of the day – the only priority, he said. It was worth studying the form.

I didn't know what I was looking for. Some of the horses were big, some were small. Some had long manes covering their eyes and others had short hair, like mine. I tried to help and pointed out one that I thought could pull a barrow. Granddad peered up from the brochure.

'Hmmph, for the money they're asking I'd expect it to build the bloody barrow!'

The only thing I knew for sure was that the whole site made the streets of Somers Town smell like a perfume factory.

After what seemed like hours of milling around and doing nothing suddenly a loud voice shouted out something I didn't catch and everyone started gravitating towards the centre of the main yard. I got there early enough to see a posh-looking man in a black suit and a top hat standing on a little raised balcony at the front. Within a couple of minutes, as the browsers assembled around us, he was lost to me behind a forest of men's legs and coats. But I knew I'd already seen the man who'd done the shouting, so when he called the morning to order at least I could picture who was saying what.

Even though I knew who was talking, once he got going I realised I couldn't understand a word he was saying. The words were pouring out of him so fast I thought at first he was speaking a foreign language.

'That's the auctioneer,' was Granddad's only explanation. He was too busy concentrating to tell me any more.

Leaving his side, I pushed my way to the edge of the crowd and found an old crate to stand on. I was hoping that watching the auctioneer would help me understand him. In fact it was more confusing. His right hand was bobbing and jerking all over the place while he rattled through what sounded like a long list of numbers. Then there was silence for a second before he smashed a black wooden hammer down on his balcony ledge. That, I did not expect.

In the short break I dived back towards Granddad and he explained more fully this time what was going on. The auctioneer was pointing at everyone who bid for the horse. The list of numbers was the price going up as a new bidder chipped in or an old one upped his offer. The hammer bang meant the horse was sold.

More informed this time, I clambered back on my crate in time to see a man in a brown overall, like the one Granddad wore in his shop, lead a horse into the yard. All the information about the horse was in the catalogue. The only thing I knew about it was that it was called 'Lot 2'.

We must have seen twenty or so horses come and go and Granddad hadn't made a single bid. Some of the lots had been donkeys, as well, so I was surprised he hadn't gone for one of those.

Lot 23 came along and at first I didn't see what the man in the overalls was leading in. Then through a gap in the crowd I spotted a little brown thing, too big to be a donkey, more like a miniature horse.

'What am I bid for this four-year-old Shetland pony?' the auctioneer said. 'Will someone give me a guinea?'

I wasn't the only one intrigued by this tiny creature. Granddad's hand shot in the air and he received a nod from the man in the top hat. I was confused. This was no donkey, even I knew that.

Three others also joined in the bidding but once it got to

eleven guineas there was only Granddad and a shorter man with a ginger moustache left. I noticed Granddad didn't look at his rival once, but Ginger couldn't stop staring across, trying to size up his opponent.

The money was going up in seven shilling instalments – a third of a guinea at a time. Twelve guineas, twelve and third, twelve and two-thirds, thirteen guineas!

I began to hope Granddad didn't win – I couldn't imagine he had enough money to pay for it.

But at fourteen guineas the auctioneer finally slammed his mallet down – and Granddad looked like he'd bought the Derby winner.

While he disappeared off to do whatever paperwork was required and, I suppose, to pay for the horse, I watched a few others go. Then I saw him emerge from the back room again and I followed him out the front. There, waiting for us, was Granddad's new Shetland pony. Close up it wasn't small at all – its ears still a couple of feet taller than my head – but it was definitely miniature compared to some of the beasts I'd seen in the Repository.

'This is Kitty,' Granddad said, introducing me. 'And Kitty, this is Alfie – he's going to walk you home.'

'But, Granddad, she's huge!'

'No, she's not. You're just smaller. But I'm assured she has a lovely temperament and, in any case, you should have pushed the barrow back last time!'

And that was it. He walked me as far as the tram station then this time there was no faking it. He climbed on the first one that came along and waved as he overtook me and Kitty walking along Blackfriars Road.

He was right, though, Kitty was no trouble. I looked forward to seeing her pull the fruit cart down to Covent Garden instead of me struggling with the hand barrow.

What I didn't know, however, was that while Kitty had been bought to pull the four-wheeled wagon, she wasn't going to be carrying fruit.

6

It's Not My Birthday

2012 was a big year for our country. Not only did London show the world that we knew how to host the Olympic Games, but it was also the year of Her Majesty's Diamond Jubilee. That, for me, was even more of a milestone because I thought the British had forgotten how to have a street party.

In 1937 we all turned out to celebrate the Coronation of George VI. What I didn't know as a kid was that it should have been a party for his brother, Edward VIII, before an affair of the heart derailed that particular project. The facts of the matter were kept from us kids. All the talk at school in the spring of 1937 was that all of Camden would be having a party!

But then I was told I wouldn't be going.

Instead, on the morning of 12 May, while the trestle tables and cockle stalls were being lined up and down Chalton Street, I found myself, along with Mum, Dad, Granddad, Grandma and a large chunk of the Dole clan, working our way down Charing Cross

Road towards Trafalgar Square, pushing through the crowds to get a view of the royal procession. I thought we were there early but the throng was six or seven deep along the route from Piccadilly. From there the royal cavalcade would head down Whitehall to Westminster Abbey. Buckingham Palace is only a hop, skip and a jump away from the Abbey but somehow they'd turned it into a six-mile journey so that more of their public could see them.

And their public had done them proud. Everyone was turned out in their Sunday best even though they must have been sweating in all those crowds. No prizes for guessing what my lot were wearing. Dad, Granddad and Grandma had polished every button and sewn up any little snags in preparation for the day. It was worth it, too. I don't know if the royal party ever saw them but hundreds of others did. As we filed our way through the bodies settling down for the day on their patch, everyone was calling out for a wave and plenty of people asked Granddad where his golden coach was.

Once again, I was envious of all the attention. Dad didn't even have to do anything. Just seeing him brought a smile to people's faces. Strangers' faces. We weren't in NW1 now. The Dole name meant nothing down here. Granddad saw me looking on.

'What's the matter, young Alfie?' he asked. 'Don't you want to see the new King and Queen?'

'Not as much as I want to be a Pearly,' I said.

'One day, young man, one day.'

The event itself passed in a sea of legs, confetti, screaming, horns being let off, and caps and hats being thrown into the air. When George and Elizabeth came close Dad scooped me and

Rosie onto his shoulders in turn. Mum stood on tiptoes with Wally and Marje on her hips. The golden coach was like something from a fairy story but what really caught my attention was the soldiers. Hundreds of men in uniform – lots of different uniforms – marching in time, some of them on horses and some of them holding swords or rifles. What seven-year-old kid wouldn't want to see that?

The ceremony itself was broadcast by the BBC and enough people around us had little portable wirelesses so we could hear every word. If anything, the noise was louder when the procession came back past us again.

It's amazing how knackering standing still all day can be. By the time we got back home that evening I was ready for a long sleep. But as we turned onto Chalton Street, the idea of going to bed left my thoughts. The street party was still in full swing – and there was jelly on some of the tables!

Thank you, King George, for that!

After a national celebration like that there was a bit of gloom over everyone for the next few days. No one was unhappy as such, but the euphoria we'd all shared had ebbed away and left the grown-ups and us kids a bit deflated. The perfect time, then, Granddad said, for the Doles to have a little knees-up.

They were all there when we arrived. Granddad, Grandma, my uncles Pat, Jim and Michael, aunts Katie, Annie, Joan and Polly, and all their own partners and children. The back room behind Granddad's fruit and veg shop at 151 Chalton Street had never been so packed.

Filing into the room in front of me, Mum and Dad made their noisy greetings. Behind them my sisters Marjorie and Rosie and brothers Wally and Dave tried to sneak in without too much attention. They just about managed it, too. Then Granddad spotted me.

'Here he is,' he bellowed. 'The star of the show!'

Me?

I froze in the doorway. All eyes darted in my direction. But why?

It's not my birthday.

I looked at Dad. He was smiling. Mum was near to tears. My brothers and sisters, like me, were just open-mouthed. They didn't have a clue what was going on either.

The room was as close to silent as it could be with so many people squeezed into it. Then Granddad stepped into the middle of the throng and beckoned me forward.

'I've got something for you, Alfie.'

Feet dragging, I stepped towards him.

'Come on, son, it's not like you to be shy,' Dad laughed. He was right. Normally I was the one told to be quiet. But this wasn't one of those times.

When I reached Granddad I noticed he had something in his hands. Something soft and shiny.

It can't be!

'You don't know how much pleasure it gives me to present you with this.'

It is.

It was a suit. Smart black trousers, a matching black jacket and pressed white shirt. But not just any suit. It was identical to the one worn by my grandfather – and that, I knew, was very special indeed. Like Granddad's, the jacket had little white buttons sewn in patterns all over the sleeves, front and back. The seams on the trousers were marked with a neat line of the gleaming plastic studs, each one lovingly hand-stitched into place by one of my relatives. I couldn't believe what I was holding.

'Is this really for me, Granddad?'

He nodded and gave me the widest smile I'd ever seen.

'Congratulations, young Alfie,' he said. 'By the power vested in me, I pronounce you a Pearly Prince of St Pancras!'

I was speechless. My tongue felt like cotton wool. All I could think, though, was, *When can I get to wear it?*

Come the following Sunday, and five or six of us were chasing an old tin can around the street. No one had replica football shirts but if we did, they'd all have said Cliff Bastin's name on the back. He was the Arsenal hero at the time, a regular goal-scoring machine according to Dad. He was the one we all pretended to be. I'd just wellied the can between the two gas streetlamps that marked our goal when Dad called out for me. I assumed our tea must be ready. With the sun shining so long each day, I had no idea of the time.

'Get yourself over to Granddad's,' Dad said. 'He's got jobs for you.'

Okay, I thought, *not tea then*. Any excuse to go over to Chalton Street was fine by me, especially if there was a shiny sovereign in it for me. Thinking about the money, I gave the can another kick and punched the air when it flew past the posts.

'Now, Alfred!' Dad boomed.

I gave the can one more almighty boot then set off. We were living in Royal College Street at the time and Chalton was about a four-minute walk. But I was seven years old. I didn't *walk* anywhere.

Being Sunday, Granddad was outside the Eastnor Castle with his seafood stall, holding court with a group of women outside his shop when I sped round the corner. He had such a gift of the gab he couldn't turn it off, even when he wasn't selling anything. I felt tired just watching him. When he saw me flump to a halt, panting out of breath, however, he broke away from his admirers.

'Here comes the worker!'

'Dad told me you had jobs,' I said.

'That's right, young man. You are going to help me win a competition.'

'What, a fruit competition?'

'Not quite. Follow me.'

Abandoning his stall – woe betide anyone who dared run off with a whelk in his absence – he marched me over to Camley Mews where I'd led Kitty the Shetland pony just weeks earlier.

Unfortunately, Kitty wasn't the only new addition to Granddad's menagerie. As well as the pigeons in the roof, two horses and a cat for ratting, he'd acquired a goat which he'd called, not unsurprisingly, Billy. Billy and I just did not get on. The first time I'd met him he'd tried to take a bite out of my hand. The same the second time and the time after that. But my fourth visit had been the worst. I was just going to give Kitty and

Tommy a stale old bun Mum had left over when I heard a hissing noise and realised Billy wasn't tied up.

And he was charging at me.

I took one look at that goat's mean eyes, caught a glimpse of his vicious-looking stumps of horn, and shinned up the lamppost in the yard as quick as any monkey in Regent's Zoo. I don't know how long I was up there before one of the neighbours heard me hollering, but I do know I ate that bun, stale as it was.

Sorry, Kitty.

Obviously that was still fresh in my mind as we approached the yard gates. I could hear Billy's bleating getting louder with every step. Although he was tethered up, I'd seen him chew through old cart tyres and a pair of boots left too close to him. A length of rope wasn't going to hold him back if he got peckish. And I got the feeling he was always peckish when he saw me.

Granddad flicked the latch, kicked the old wooden door open then laughed, watching me flinch. Granddad noticed it too. He walked in, over the straw-covered cobbles, and stopped about two foot from the end of Billy's rope.

'Now, about that job, young Alfie.'

'Yes?' I said, my eyes never leaving that damned goat.

'I need you to give old Billy a bath.'

It took a few seconds to sink in. When it did, my face must have been a picture.

'Granddad . . . I . . . Billy – no!'

Then I saw the big grin on Granddad's face and I knew he was joking. 'Okay,' he said, 'the bath can wait – *for now*. Maybe you can help me get Kitty ready instead.'

'Ready for what, Granddad?' I asked.

'Ready for her big day out.'

Like all Shetlands, Kitty wasn't tall by any means, but I still needed a chair to reach over her. Balancing a bucket of soapy water on a low wall, Granddad showed me how to douse her thick brown coat then scrub away at it as hard as I could.

'Won't I hurt her?' I asked.

'She'll soon let you know if you do.'

That filled me with confidence. I thought about the heavy iron ring in the wall that she was tied to and hoped it would hold, especially with me overstretching to reach everywhere. I had no idea if I was making any difference but Granddad seemed to think it was okay. Pulling up a crate, he reached into his pocket and produced the familiar silver snuff box. Clearly he wasn't planning on helping me out any time soon.

I said I was overstretching and I said the bucket was balanced on a wall. Well, obviously the inevitable happened. When Granddad looked up I was lying on the floor, the chair on its side, and both Kitty and I were drenched.

'Well, that's one way of doing it!' For a minute I thought I saw Granddad reaching for his belt but in fact he was just getting a little rubber brush.

'Now, have you ever used a curry comb before?'

I shook my head.

'Well, you're going to now.'

Fixing the strap on the back of the brush over his hand, Granddad dragged the comb over Kitty's coat, its hard rubber nubbins squeezing the soap and water and any dirt out onto the floor. I watched as he moved the comb in long, equal strokes.

'Now I'm going to leave you to it,' he said, adjusting the strap to fix my hand, 'so try not to get distracted this time.' Then, when he reached the yard door, he added, 'Billy could still do with that bath, you know . . .'

I don't know how Kitty stood me mucking about around her, but she was as good as gold. Maybe she even liked the curry comb being dragged down her. I did. It was strangely satisfying feeling the rubber bristles come across a knot or loose hair or piece of mud, and run it all out onto the floor. I was so wrapped up in brushing and teasing and grooming her, that I didn't even notice Billy gnawing his way through another rope. And, when I did, I didn't care.

I was looking after Kitty and she would look after me. At least, that's what I hoped.

Satisfied that the curry comb had done its job, next I got hold of a normal brush and started going over the same areas again. I couldn't remember the last time I ever put so much care into something.

'I'm going to get you looking fit for a king,' I whispered into her long, alert ears. Then I giggled. 'A Pearly King.'

While I was desperate to get Kitty looking her beautiful best, I also wanted to please my grandfather, of course I did. I wanted to see that big smile break out across his ruddy face and have him ruffle my hair in pride.

Which is exactly what happened.

'Oh, Alfie, Alfie,' he said when he came back. 'You've done

our Kitty proud.' He ran his hand lovingly down the horse's long nose then patted her flank. 'She's never looked more beautiful, young man. Well done.'

If I thought that was the end of it, I was mistaken. Kitty's hooves still needed a buff so, with Granddad whispering sweet nothings into the horse's ears, I knelt on the cobbles and nervously began to scrape a file over the right front hoof. Granddad promised Kitty wouldn't feel a thing as I began chipping off all the specks of straw and mud from her foot, but I was just reaching round the far side when she picked her leg up and stamped down hard.

Just missing my supporting hand.

'Flaming hell, Granddad!' I screamed. 'She could have crushed me.'

'All the more reason to hurry up then,' he said cheerily. Then, handing me a chamois leather to complete the job, he added, 'I want to see my face in those hooves.'

If she moves like that again, it'll be my face you'll see in them.

By the time I'd finished, I was no longer intimidated by the powerful legs that could break my bones with one skittish kick. The only thing I cared about was buffing those hooves until they gleamed. Whatever Granddad wanted Kitty ready for, she was just about there. The old man agreed. As I stood up and stretched the aches out of my body, he produced a tangerine from his pocket and said, 'You've done a sterling job, Alfie. Now, you'd better get yourself home and dried and into bed.'

Maybe he saw the look on my face at the sight of just a tangerine.

'Oh, and you'd better have this as well,' he said, and pressed a shilling into my palm.

'I'll give you half a crown if you do Billy next time?'

'Er, no thanks, Granddad. See you in the morning!'

It wasn't unusual for me to be up at six o'clock on a Monday. But it was unusual on a bank holiday, especially for Mum to be standing over me, comb and grease in her hands, trying to bully my hair into some sort of order. I swear she was harder on me than I'd been on Kitty. After a few minutes she stood back, finally satisfied.

'You'll do,' she said. 'Now, there's just one more thing.'

She marched out of the room and into hers. When she returned a minute later, she was carrying a suit. *The* suit. The one that was identical to Dad's and Granddad's.

The one covered in little white buttons.

Finally I was going to get to wear it.

7

What are You Having,
Your Majesty?

For as long as I could remember, the annual London Cart Horse Parade was held in Regent's Park every Whit Monday. Anyone from the capital's boroughs with a working animal was invited to show their steed and compete for one of the day's prizes. I knew Granddad George entered it every year, like many costers did with their donkeys. But this was the first time Kitty had ever been shown.

And the first time I'd been invited to tag along. In my suit!

I'd been on the cart dozens of times, accompanying Granddad down to Covent Garden market for a particularly large load and sometimes on family outings, but never like this. Up front, even at seven o'clock in the morning, Granddad was dressed in his full Pearly uniform. The black coat tails, suit trousers, waistcoat and hat, all covered in white buttons – each one lovingly sewn on by his own hand. Next to him, Grandma Emma looked a million dollars in her matching ensemble. Her hat was bigger than Granddad's, with a long white feather waving proudly from side to side as the cart lurched down the street. On the back of her coat, picked out in shiny mother-of-pearl buttons, there was a message.

'Pearly Queen of St Pancras'.

I looked over to Granddad. On his back, above the large picture of a cartwheel, it read, 'Pearly King of St Pancras'. Next to me, in his matching outfit, I knew without looking what Dad's buttoned label said because on my own back it said the same thing.

'Pearly Prince of St Pancras'.

I had never felt so proud.

The southeast corner of Regent's Park was less than a mile away. Early though it was, we'd barely turned on to the Euston Road before I saw the first cart heading in the same direction. Then the second, and the third. Fourth, fifth, sixth and dozens and dozens more. Every time I blinked more seemed to appear. As I looked behind us, past the giant gasometers looming over from York Way, I saw the snake of carts stretching down the Gray's Inn Road, past the old Victoria Hotel – now the McDonald's opposite King's Cross Station – past the glamorous Regent Cinema opposite St Pancras, and past the coach station on the corner of Judd Street. It was much the same story up ahead. Not far in front of us, a 218 double-decker trolley bus sat empty, its passengers having long since hopped off the back to walk more quickly than the horse-drawn traffic jam would allow. I could see the conductor hanging off the pole at the back. He wasn't going to take much money today, that much was obvious to both of us.

Everywhere I looked, they were there, carts of all shapes and sizes picking their way through the tramlines and trolley buses and the occasional car. And they were all heading to the same place as us.

That's when I started to worry. Because that's when I realised that each of the hundreds of wooden carts trundling along was being pulled by an immaculately groomed horse. Some of the other beasts were huge, dwarfing poor little Kitty. But whatever their size, they were all dressed to the nines with ribbons and coloured bridles decorated with brass. It was a wonderful sight but I couldn't relax.

I bet they weren't prepared by a kid who didn't know what he was doing.

Luckily, Granddad didn't seem too concerned by the competition.

'They're nice,' he roared above the din of clip-clops on the tarry block road surface, 'but they're not Pearlies!'

I folded my arms, feeling the firm round buttons under my hands, and looked at the similarly ornate designs on Kitty's reins.

No, they're not, I thought. *No, they're not.*

The Regent's Park parade had been running for as long as Granddad had been in London, attracting more than a thousand four-legged competitors in the years before the Great War. In the intervening decades the advent of motor vehicles had made a dent in numbers but it didn't feel like it. Animal traffic jams spread as far as the eye could see in all directions as hundreds and hundreds of smartly dressed families made their way to the Park's Outer Circle. And they were just the competitors. Ten times that amount of people were already filing their way in every available entrance, every single person done up in their bank holiday best. And all of them gave us a wave. Among the amazing bold colours of the horses and carts and their owners surrounding us, it was the black and white splendour of the Dole carriage that caught the eye.

Aunt Annie didn't go out as much as the others but even without her, Granddad, Grandma and Dad milked the attention like the experienced performers they were. I'd seen them all work their charms collecting for charity around the pubs and entertainment halls of north London, teasing pennies and more from drinkers and landlords alike. Everyone had time for a Pearly, Granddad used to say, and I'd seen it often enough with my own eyes. But seeing was one thing. Now I was experiencing it myself.

'Look, there's a little Pearly on the back!' one lady's voice called out, and before I knew it there were dozens of arms waving in my direction, all trying to shake my hand as Kitty slowly joined the procession into the park. I looked at Dad next to me, who could not have had a wider smile.

'Go on, son,' he said, 'you'll make their day.'

So there I was, seven years old, leaning over the side of Granddad's old grocery cart, pressing the flesh with smiling strangers who couldn't stop marvelling at my finery. They didn't know me from Adam but everyone I spoke to was bowled over by the sight of a young Pearly. I'd always known it was a heritage

I'd been honoured to grow up part of. But this was the first time I'd experienced the universal goodwill people seemed to have towards the buttons. I'd never felt prouder in my life.

It was ten o'clock before we finally reached the place Granddad had been heading for. As far as I could tell it was just a continuation of the traffic jam, there were so many horses and carts nose to tail. But all the drivers seemed to be standing alongside their wagons and there was a real party atmosphere among them. If they didn't know each other to begin with, they soon did after so long staring at each other's backs queuing up to get in. It took Granddad precisely two seconds to have a small crowd around him as, ever the gent, he held out his hand and escorted his Queen down the steps to terra firma once more. Grandma was even more of a draw than her husband, and she soon had everyone laughing at some story or other. Dad and I watched from the sidelines.

'Your time will come,' he said, pinching my cheek. 'Mine too, for that matter.'

With so many hundreds of horses around, it was going to be hours until Kitty and Granddad began competing for anything, so Dad said I could go for a wander if I wanted.

Wanted? I couldn't wait. And I knew exactly where to head.

I'd spied the bandstand on the way in and even though we'd gone a fair way past, I could still hear the music ringing out. It was a warm day so everyone was hot in their suits, but by the time I tracked the source of the swing jazz sounds down, couples were already dancing. I had no interest in dancing of any kind, I just wanted to see the band. The parties at Granddad's house always ended up with some sort of impromptu jam. Someone always jumped on the piano, there were usually a couple of fiddlers in the group, and Granddad was a demon on the spoons. But this was different. These were professional musicians, following music and singing too. I was mesmerised.

It wasn't just my eyes and ears that were being treated, though. The sweetest smell I'd ever experienced was wafting in from somewhere. The moment the band announced they were taking a break, I decided to follow my nose. Pushing through the crowds wasn't easy, especially being the level of most people's backsides, but I didn't need to see where I was going.

I'd never seen a chestnut stall before. By coincidence, the owner had never seen a Pearly Prince, either. So that was a first for both of us.

'What are you having, your majesty?' the man asked.

'Oh, nothing for me,' I said. 'I haven't got any money. I just wanted to see where the nice smell was coming from.'

The man shook his head and looked around at the queue of people waiting for his next batch.

'Wait there,' he said. 'We can't have a Pearly going hungry, can we?'

A few minutes later I was clutching my own cone of the sweetest and hottest treats I'd ever tasted and I knew I had my suit to thank.

Which reminded me: *Granddad!*

In all the excitement of the bandstand I'd forgotten the time. Granddad was due to compete at midday. I had no idea what time it was but the sun was pretty high above so if it wasn't twelve already then it couldn't be far off.

Sweating and out of breath, I found Dad with Grandma leaning against a tree a few yards back from the performance area.

'You're just in time, Boy-Boy,' Grandma said.

'You're right about that, Mum,' Dad said. 'Give us a chestnut, son – I'm starving!'

Somehow above the din of the crowd I heard a man with a megaphone announce that the next competitor was a local celebrity.

'Ladies and Gentlemen, competitor number three-seven-six, George Dole and Kitty!'

Dad had to put me on his shoulders to see – which meant taking his jacket off so I didn't destroy the buttons – but I was so glad he did. There was a fifty-yard area pegged out, and Granddad was leading his trusty Shetland around the perimeter, then back into the centre. There were even a few cones to weave around, which they navigated perfectly. I'm not sure how much credit went to Granddad – he seemed to be more interested in waving to the crowd. But Kitty knew where she was going.

Afterwards Granddad pulled up alongside three men with clipboards.

'They're the judges,' Dad called up. 'I hope you polished those bloody hooves.'

If he was worried, I was mortified. Was some judge really going to check my work? I couldn't believe Granddad had entrusted me with such an important job. But checking they were. Scrutinising, in fact. While one man gave the cart the once-over, another walked his way alongside Kitty, running his hands down her coat, and feeling the brushed hair and her combed mane. The third looked like he was making notes about the button-embellished bridle and reins before dropping to his haunches and tapping one of Kitty's feet.

I thought I was going to pass out. What if they found something I'd missed?

A few minutes later, to a resounding cheer from the crowd, Granddad leaped back on board the cart and led Kitty back to the parking area. He'd done his best. Now it was up to the judges. Unfortunately they still had another fifty to get through in his category.

'How long are they going to take?' I asked Dad.

'As long as they have to,' he said. 'Go and find the zoo or the lake for an hour or two. It's not worth hanging around here.'

By the time I reached the outskirts of the zoo's grounds, there were already dozens of kids who'd had the same idea. The moment one of them spotted me, I felt like I was behind the fence with the lions and giraffes. Before I knew it, there was a circle around me. It wasn't threatening but I wasn't comfortable either. They only wanted to touch my suit and ask me about it but I didn't have the answers. I suppose I came from a very small world. Without transport and communications, you only ever really know the people you see every day and I was used to everyone knowing about the Pearlies.

I didn't have a clue what I was meant to say when a boy asked me what my buttons meant. That was a mistake I promised myself I'd rectify as soon as I found my granddad again.

What was the point in dressing the part if I didn't know what it stood for?

All thoughts of my heritage soon left my head as the other kids lost interest and we all started chasing around the wire fences looking for new and wilder animals to mimic among ourselves. Then at three o'clock I decided to head back. I don't know how I found my family again, but the stench of the horses' poo certainly led me in the right direction.

'Did we win?' I asked Grandma.

'We're about to find out,' she replied. 'Look.'

The three judges from earlier were all sitting on a raised plinth. Another man at a table was writing things down. Alongside them was the announcer. His loudhailer was poised to go to his lips as soon as the verdict came in.

'Granddad's definitely going to win!' I announced. 'Kitty's the best horse in the world.'

'That she may be,' Dad said calmly. 'But there were a few decent shows after you left. Those judges'll have their work cut out today.'

It hadn't occurred to me that Granddad wouldn't win. Looking at the worried expression on Dad's face and noticing the way Grandma was twirling her handkerchief between her hands told me they weren't so confident. That, in turn, made me feel sick to the stomach. I suddenly wished I could run over with the curry comb and make sure Kitty's coat was gleaming.

There was a buzz around the huge crowd as the judges all sat back and nodded at the man with the pen. He said something to the announcer and passed over a sheet of paper.

'Here we go,' Dad said. 'Fingers crossed, son.'

'In third place,' the tinny loudhailer's voice said, 'is Bert Grey and Melody.'

A huge cheer erupted from somewhere over to my left. It quickly died out but not before drowning out the announcement about second place.

'Who did he say?' Grandma shouted anxiously.

'I don't know,' Dad said. 'Maybe we should—'

He stopped. The announcer was speaking again.

'And in first place, the judges have voted for . . .' he paused for dramatic effect. 'George Dole and Kitty!'

It was a slow-motion moment and not just for me. It seemed to take an age for the words to sink into my brain and, judging by how late Dad was in scooping me up into the air, he'd taken his time translating the result as well. Around us, a vast circle of well-wishers formed, quickly doubling when people noticed our suits matched that of the man in the winner's enclosure. A couple of men tried to pick Grandma up to join me at shoulder height, but she wouldn't hear of it. Instead, we all pushed our way through the crowd to the front where Granddad was waiting proudly by his cart.

'Come on then, you lot,' he called out. 'We've got a medal to collect.'

If all eyes had been on us when we'd arrived, now it literally felt like being under a giant microscope as Granddad clicked his tongue and Kitty began the slow hike over to where the judges were waiting. Either side of us, the audience formed a narrow human corridor. They all reached forward and banged the side of the cart in support, or reached out to shake our hands. I was so glad I was protected by my family and the wagon's low walls. That experience at the zoo had shaken me.

By the time we pulled to a halt alongside the raised judging area, the cheering was deafening. Granddad had been a popular winner. Or maybe it was Kitty. How many people had seen a Pearly Pony before?

There was an almighty burst of applause as the gold rosette with the massive '1st' in its centre was attached to Kitty's bridle. Instinctively Dad and Granddad stood up and threw their hats into the air. Luckily for both, they landed back on the cart. That's when I realised how much it meant to them to win. And how much the Pearlies meant to the whole crowd.

As we made our way slowly back home, I realised it wasn't just important to the hundreds of strangers who'd cheered Kitty's victory. The next occasion when I got to wear my suit couldn't come quickly enough.

Not for the Pearly Prince of St Pancras.

8

Give Us A Twirl

'Go on, son. In you go.'

I felt the nudge in my back but I didn't move. Not an inch. The nudge was heavier the second time and the voice had an edge.

'For God's sake, Boy-Boy, just go through the bloody door.'

I turned and looked up into my dad's face. Seeing my anxiety, he smiled, the lightness back in his tone again.

'You've been looking forward to this all day. Come on, I'm right behind you.'

'Can't you go first?' I begged.

'Of course I can. But then no one will see you. And what's the point of that? You're the star turn tonight. I want to show you off to the world.'

The world I was happy with. After the big day out in Regent's Park I'd got a taste for people looking at me and admiring my suit. But they were strangers. There were millions of them, all faceless. Whereas behind the frosted-glass saloon doors of this little pub in north London I would most likely find a collection of aunts, uncles, neighbours, shopkeepers, parents of my friends – basically the faces I saw every day – I lived, as I remembered again, in a very small world. And it was Saturday night, after all.

Even if they weren't here in the Neptune, they'd be up the road in the Cock or the Eastnor Castle – and we were heading to those next.

I realised I was shivering. Cold or nerves? Well, it was mid-June so it wasn't the temperature. I knew there was a roaring fire in each bar on the other side of those dark walls. What was I waiting for? I pushed against the glass then felt it swing open as Dad's hand reached over my head to hold the door steady.

The warmth hit me first. Then the noise.

Then the silence.

For what felt like minutes the only sound coming from anywhere was the crackling of the logs in the hearth where a couple of lads were roasting nuts. Then a familiar voice sang out.

'Look at the little fella!' the barmaid squealed. 'He's got a pearly suit like his old man.'

That was my cue. I'm not saying Dad pushed me but a few seconds later I found myself struggling for balance bang in the middle of the room and the place had erupted. Everyone wanted to see my buttons.

'Aw, bless 'im,' a woman said. 'He looks a lot cuter than you do in your suit, Alf.'

'He looks a lot cuter than you 'n' all, Sally,' Dad laughed. I saw him get a playful whack for his cheek, relieved at least two pairs of eyes were no longer focused entirely on me. The respite didn't last long.

'Let's get a proper look at you then, boy,' a man said, and suddenly two big hands tucked under my arms and scooped me up until I was standing on the bar itself. A chorus of wolf-whistles and cheers swept the room. I felt my cheeks burning and it had nothing to do with the fire.

'Give us a twirl!' someone called out.

I shot a look at my dad. He laughed and stretched out his arm.

'Spin round, lad, and let everyone see your mum's handiwork.'

Gingerly I started to turn.

'Not so fast!' called out the landlord. 'It's not a bloomin' carousel.'

'You leave him alone.' The woman called Sally shot him down. 'You're doing fine, love.'

I didn't feel fine. It was bad enough being in the spotlight. Having to pick my way round damp beer towels and empty ale jars on the sticky surface was terrifying. What if I fell? What if I broke something? Dad wouldn't be happy.

But he looked content enough right then.

I wished I could say the same about myself. As one person after another called out to me to give them a smile or a wave or to comment on my outfit, I just wanted to jump down and run out of the bar. I thought I'd wanted this. I'd been so proud to get my suit I couldn't wait to show it off. Granddad said it would be fun. He said I'd get a kick out of helping people. That I'd be a natural Pearly Prince.

He was wrong.

'I want to go home, Dad,' I said.

Somehow, above the din of the crowd returning to their drinks and shouted conversations, Dad heard me. He hadn't left my side.

'You can go home in a minute if you want,' he whispered. 'But first you need to just hold this for me.'

It was an old tin cup. I'd been told what to do with it but knowing and doing were two different things. People were already beginning to turn away from me. If the moment hadn't already gone it was certainly beginning to pack its bags.

'You'll be fine, son. Trust me.' I took Dad's outstretched hands and jumped down from the bar. Within a second I heard the tinkle of a shilling being put into the cup.

'Who could say no to such a smart little chap?'

I recognised the speaker as Mr Jacobs the haberdasher and went to smile a 'thank you'. Before I could do it another coin hit the cup. Then another. And another. Someone put a hand on my shoulder and guided me over to the furthest table where a couple of smart ladies were holding court surrounded by what looked like a guard of men.

'Oh, look,' one of the women said, 'who could resist such a little sweetheart?'

No sooner had she spoken than all the men in her group fished into their pockets and produced handfuls of coins. I couldn't help but grin, even when one of the men took off my cap to tousle my hair. I was doing it. I was collecting money. Granddad's charities would be getting a bonanza tonight.

And I was enjoying it.

When a friend of my Aunt Annie asked me for a joke I told her one. It wasn't great, but she laughed like a drain. When another lady with glasses and smudged lipstick wondered if I knew any songs, I gave her a chorus of 'Muffin Man'. I was getting into it. Just like Granddad had said I would. I was being a proper Pearly Prince. I couldn't wait to tell him.

I never actually got the chance.

'The boy's a natural!' the familiar voice boomed out.

'Granddad!'

If I thought I'd made an entrance, he more than topped it. His sheer girth alone filled the Neptune's double doors. He was an imposing presence that couldn't help command the room. While everyone stopped their chatter to welcome him in, and compliment him on a terrific turn from his grandson – *me* – I just ran up and leaped into his arms.

'How's my little Prince getting on?' Without waiting for a reply he lifted the tin mug from my hand and laughed.

'You've earned more in ten minutes that I get all night! Maybe you should be the Pearly King of St Pancras and not me!'

Getting a free glass of lemonade and an arrowroot biscuit from every pub I went to was pretty good payment just for wearing my favourite outfit and I couldn't wait to do it again. Making Granddad proud for once also gave me a warm feeling inside, but it was good to see Dad let his hair down as well. I'd noticed that he'd started to work longer hours and then hit the pub most nights afterwards. That wasn't his way, not normally. Once or twice I heard raised voices from the front room when he and Mum got a bit heated in their conversation.

'Where's your backbone, Alfie Dole?' Mum was shouting. 'You should just tell him it's not on. Look at your health.'

I didn't catch Dad's reply but I could tell he wanted Mum to drop it. When I asked her what it was all about she told me it wasn't anything for me to worry about. But, she added, 'If your dad doesn't start doing fewer hours he'll end up on the sick bed.'

After that, of course, I was looking for signs of Dad's deteriorating health every time I saw him. I suppose he did get more ratty – or rather, less patient – with us kids, so we felt his tongue more than usual. And arguments between him and Mum began to happen more often, only now they didn't bother hiding away in the front room.

When summer arrived it was usual for Dad to have his shirt off around the house. The rest of us did, it was so stifling. For some reason this year he kept it on. Then one day I caught sight of him in the tin bath we had in the kitchen. His back was red raw. In fact it was hurting him to try even to clean it, let alone dry it with one of our rough towels. When he saw my face he told me it wasn't as bad as it looked. It's just he'd got a temporary job carrying cement for bricklayers on a building site and it was hard work. He had to lug a hundredweight a go and half the time it had just come out the kiln so his back would burn. Between the weight and the heat his back had burned, bled and blistered every day for weeks.

Now I knew what Mum had been arguing with him about.

Still, for a kid, out of sight really is out of mind and as it was summer, I was spending most of the time outside so I saw Dad less and less. Anyway, worrying about him wasn't my main concern when there was exploring to do. Mum didn't really mind what I got up to as long as I didn't go far. But she never said where 'far' began and I pretended not to know. A couple of times I ended up with mates at Regent's Canal in Camden or on the other side behind King's Cross and a voice in the back of my head told me I shouldn't tell Mum. I had a pretty good idea what she'd do if she knew her seven-year-old was messing around with the locks and chasing narrow boats along the towpath. I knew I'd have fun there when I was older, though.

In summer Mum's market business boomed as people wanted cold salads for their tea. I had to help Dad carry home double the amounts of beetroot and celery and onions and then, if she needed to have Walter with her, I'd have to go along with Mum on a Sunday to help her sell it or keep the toddler entertained, whatever was easier for her.

I remember one week playing with Wally just along from Mum. She was standing under the shop canopy to keep the sun off her face but kids don't know about shade. She'd told me to make sure Wally kept his little shirt on, so I guess it was hot enough to burn, but I was in my shorts and scuffed-up shoes and loving every minute of it.

Suddenly there was a crash from behind me. When I looked over, Mum's salads were all over the floor where she'd barged past the barrow in a hurry. Next thing I heard was her shouting and then I saw her launch herself at this big guy in a three-piece suit. I didn't have a clue who he was but he knew who Mum was. She was smacking him viciously and when he blocked her with his thick arm she made a grab for his beard instead. It was like she was possessed.

To his credit, the man defended himself as best he could but never retaliated. The crowd that had quickly formed around them might have put him off. Eventually, though, Mum was pulled away by another trader and told to sort herself out. But she couldn't leave without spitting on the boots of the man she'd attacked.

'If he gets sick, I'll be coming for you. That's a promise.'

Afterwards, as I helped her pick up the celery and everything else, I plucked up the courage to ask who the man was.

'He's the so-and-so who's going to drive your father into an early grave with his work,' she said, still out of breath. 'How dare he show his face near me.'

He won't make that mistake again, I thought. *But*, I wondered, *how's Dad going to like Mum trying to beat up his boss?*

The answer was there to see – or rather hear – that night. Of course, his boss had had words and Dad was ashamed that Mum had got involved. But maybe she'd helped matters because, he said, he was being given a few days' holiday.

'So it looks like I can come hopping with you after all!'

9

That Carpet Just Moved

The first time I heard the word 'hopping' was in the middle of summer when Aunt Annie told Mum, 'Alf, Rosie and Dave will need to get their hopping letters from Dr Shaw.'

I wasn't meant to be earwigging so I didn't say anything, not even to my brother and sister. A few days later Mum marched us round to Little Drummond Street and the GP surgery housed there. After Mum signed us in, Dave said, 'Why are we here, Mum? There's nothing wrong with us.'

'Yes, but there needs to be.'

All was explained when we went in and a lady introduced herself as Dr Shaw. When she asked what she could do for us, Mum started to say that we were planning to go hopping that August. She didn't need to finish the sentence.

'I think that's a marvellous idea, Mrs Dole,' the doctor said. 'Your children don't look well at all. I should consider it essential for their health that they enjoy a stint in the countryside.'

Without another word she scribbled on several pieces of paper then handed them over.

'There you go,' she said, addressing us kids this time. 'Three letters excusing you from school on medical grounds. Now have a lovely time!'

Letters excusing us from school? Written by a doctor? Just so we could go to the countryside? My mind boggled at the time but I can see Dr Shaw's point. She wasn't on the take, if that's what you're thinking. No one was bribing her for these letters. She genuinely believed that two, three, sometimes four to six weeks away from London, or at least our pocket of it, would be of benefit to our health, so much so that she was prepared to waive the education system's rights over us for a couple of months. The smog, the smoking, the close contact with so many other people, many of them not in the best of health themselves, the poor drainage, the rubbish and animal excrement on the streets and the emerging presence of combustion engine exhaust fumes couldn't compare to blue skies and fresh air. Back then, though, I didn't know I was living under such bad conditions because I'd never known anything else.

Not even for a single day.

The closest I'd come to outside London was crossing the river to Elephant. The closest I'd come to countryside was the Royal Parks. But, do you know what, you don't miss what you've never had. And you definitely don't miss it if you've never heard of it.

As for 'hopping' itself, if it had nothing to do with bouncing on one leg then I was stumped. Mum wasn't going to tell me, either.

'You'll see when we get there,' she said, grinning. 'It's a surprise.'

I don't know if that's a good thing or a bad thing . . .

The sound and smell of steam trains was a massive part of my childhood, always in the background wherever I lived. I took their whistles and chugs through the night in my stride and I even liked the clouds of the smoke that drifted past us, depending on the wind. But there was one thing about them I didn't know: what they were like to travel on.

Depending on where we were living at the time, I could probably have hit St Pancras or King's Cross or Euston with a stone if I'd tried, and yet I'd never set foot inside one of those giant steel horses. I'd had no cause. Everyone I knew lived within half a mile of us. Why would we ever go anywhere else?

The answer was: because everyone else was coming too.

It wasn't the entire Dole operation by any means but there were enough of us filing into London Bridge to fill an entire modern carriage. Unfortunately, compartments were smaller back then and most of them were already half occupied by the time we started boarding. That wasn't good enough for Dad. He ran the full length of the platform searching for a vacant one. He succeeded, but we were barely inside when it quickly filled with strangers. That was going to make things interesting . . .

As the train pulled out of London Bridge, the other kids in our carriage were cooing at the buildings passing by. Some things never change, and the view of London from a train track remains as unique today as it was then. The lines are like arteries through to the heart of the capital, taking you up close to sights you don't normally witness.

Unfortunately, I didn't see any of it.

There was a reason Dad wanted an empty carriage. It was because he had a piece of cargo that he wanted to get up on the luggage rack before anyone else got in the way. It was an old hessian grain sack with a rug inside. But that wasn't all. Wrapped up inside the mat was yours truly. It was the only way my parents could think of saving a fare, and I was the only one who was young enough to fit but old enough not to make a fuss.

'It's only an hour's journey,' Dad had said. 'Your cousins will be doing it as well. Just don't move.'

So there I was, pretending to be a carpet, having to listen to the squeals of kids loving the views. Worst of all, I could hear my brothers and sisters having fun as well. The only way I kept myself going was the satisfaction of knowing Wally would soon be big enough to travel like this as well.

I actually got quite comfortable on the shelf and found myself nearly nodding off a couple of times. At some point I must have given in and let my brain switch off because the next thing I knew I'd jolted back to life and the only thing I could hear was a kid's voice.

'I swear, Dad, that carpet just moved!'

I must have tossed or turned over in my sleep but luckily only the kid, a young one by the sound of it, saw it. I knew his excitable tone from experience. It was the voice that goes higher and higher with exasperation, the one we use when adults won't believe us.

Then another voice I didn't recognise spoke.

'It's just the motion of the train, Bobby.'

Thank the Lord for the relentless logic of parents.

Thanks to my forty winks I lost track of how long we'd been travelling. But I knew which station to listen out for and eventually I heard the Tannoy calling it out.

'Paddock Wood. This is Paddock Wood. All passengers for Paddock Wood alight here.'

Unfortunately the other families in our carriage were staying on for the coast so I couldn't relax. I felt Dad grab hold of the sack from each end then, as I held my breath, he hoisted me down, half-cursing as he did. Then he slung me over his shoulder and I bounced along through what I imagined to be the station, although it was a lot quieter than London Bridge. That was my first clue that the countryside was going to be different.

I spent a good few minutes flapping along on Dad's shoulder, then he stopped. By now there were loads of other voices nearby, many I recognised.

'Down you come, then,' Dad said, and I felt my heart hit my mouth as he swooped me off his back and planted me on the ground so I was actually on my feet. As he loosened the sack, my carpet prison began to unfold and within a couple of seconds it had completely fallen away. Around me my cousins and aunts and uncles were laughing at the magic act. I didn't care. I was too busy staring past them. For as far as I could see there was grass of all heights and shades, and trees and animals. There were cows and sheep and somewhere there must have been an aviary because the noise of birds was piercing. A winding lane led round past the trees to God knows where.

I hadn't seen this coming. I hadn't been able to see anything. Where had my city gone? Where were the streets packed with houses? Where were the costers and hawkers chasing passers-by? Where was the *noise*?

I'd moved house half a dozen times so that wasn't the problem. The problem was: there were no houses.

'I don't like it, Dad,' I said. 'I want to go home.'

We walked along that lane for about a mile. At some point I realised there were a lot more people than just my family surrounding us. Wherever we were going, it was popular.

The more we walked, however, the more I got into it. I loved being in Regent's Park and this was no different really, except the grass was longer and there were trees everywhere you looked instead of here and there. After fifteen minutes I couldn't remember why I'd been upset in the first place.

While the adults followed the path, me and my cousins ran alongside in the shrubs and bushes. It was good to see everyone having fun together. I asked one of them whether he'd come down on the luggage rack as well.

'No? I had a seat. Didn't you?'

It turned out no one else had been stuffed inside a sack and told to play dead for an hour. *Nice one, Dad.*

Suddenly there was a holler from outside the wood. When I went out I saw that Dad and the rest had stopped. 'Here we are,' he said.

Here? I thought. *Where's here?*

I left my cousins for dead and pushed past all the stationary adult legs. I needed to see this new home in the middle of nowhere for myself.

At first I thought Dad was having a giraffe (*laugh*) but the way my cousins just cheered and ran full pelt forwards I knew he wasn't. But where were they running to? All I could see was a field with a bunch of sheds on it. There wasn't a brick in sight.

Those 'sheds' would later become the one place in the world that I would always think of as 'home', but as a kid transported out of a city for the first time in my life, I was just perplexed. I'd never seen anything like it.

The field, or 'common' as Dad called it, had rows of huts on either side. Each hut was about ten foot by eight and they ran in groups of six, then there was a hut's-width break, then another half-dozen. Attached to the back of each hut there was another one facing in the opposite direction. On the other side of the common the pattern was repeated so, in total, there were forty-eight little boxes, each one packed to the walls with a family. At the far end of the block were two separate wooden huts. From the line of people waiting outside I knew they were toilets. Maybe this wasn't going to be so different from London after all.

Our hut faced towards the centre of the common. Like all the others it was made of tin with a flat corrugated roof. Inside there was just one room with a load of straw and bundles of faggots – sticks – in the corner. That was it. I expected Kitty to appear at any moment. This was just like her stable, except smaller. Where was the furniture? Where would we put our clothes? And where were we going to sleep?

The last question was answered when Mum produced what looked like several sheets stitched together from the corner of the room.

'Right,' she said to me, Rosie and David, 'see all that straw?' She pointed at what looked like cattle feed. 'That needs to be stuffed inside this mattress case. We'll be sleeping on that tonight.'

She also had five pillowcases for us to fill as well. For the first time in my life I found myself wondering what a real pillow has inside it. It couldn't really be these crackly little sticks, could it? Surely I would have noticed.

What started as a chore became a game the second Mum and Marjorie left the hut. Suddenly I got a face full of straw from David, Rosie had it stuffed down her back by me and poor little Wally had a pillowcase thrown over his head before being launched onto the faggots. Of course, when Mum came back it was all done and the mattress was in place. Only the sight of hay peeping out of Wally's nappy and shirt made her suspicious. But we'd done our bit so she told us to clear off until dinner.

Now this was what I called a holiday. All my anxiety from earlier vanished the second I was let off the leash. I couldn't wait to run around the open fields and explore. A bit of an ordeal had just become an adventure.

In the middle of the common there was a standpipe and a queue of people waiting with bottles and tubs to fill. Even though it was sunny, and had been every day for weeks, the little patch underneath the tap was already a muddy pool. I knew what I'd be playing in later.

Beyond the common and past the other line of huts there were fields and fields of crops. Some of them were knee-high and reminded me of the things Granddad bought at Covent Garden market. Other things I'd never seen before, especially the ones that seemed to my young eyes to be snaking magically up into the sky. On closer inspection I discovered it was less like magic and more like an actual factory out in the open air. At the edges of the field there were thick wooden columns, like telegraph poles, and from the top of these a network of cables crisscrossed the field in parallel lines. Each cable had lengths of binding hanging down the fifteen feet or so to the ground and it was up this binding that the plants had wound themselves. That's why they looked like they were flying, but for a kid it was still like being in the story of *Jack and the Beanstalk*. Any one of those vines could have an ogre at the top.

If I thought that was weird, getting to the end of the field there seemed to be a circus going on. There were about a dozen men all balancing on thick, wooden stilts, staggering along the rows of cable, cutting down the bindings from where they were suspended at the top. Another guy below scooped the whole snake up and piled it in a barrow. When that was full, another man dragged it away and they started filling another. I was mesmerised by it all. I kept waiting for one of the stilt-walkers to topple down when they wobbled but it never happened.

The aroma coming from the plants was unlike anything I'd ever come across. It was sweet and acrid at the same time. I could feel it in my lungs, just sitting at the side. This, I heard one of the men say, was the hops field.

So this is what we've come here for?

Between the fields and the common was a funny-looking house – funny because it didn't have any other houses joined on to it. My reading wasn't very good but I could make out a sign at the front which read 'Bore Green Farm'.

I'd guessed it was a farm but seeing the name just left me more in the dark. We weren't farmers, none of us were. Only Granddad knew his way around fruit and veg and he wasn't here. So what did this Bore Green Farm have to do with us?

The thought didn't stay with me long because there was still plenty to explore. By the time we'd found the lake and the river and climbed as many trees as we could it was getting dark. In summer that meant it was gone eight o'clock. That was the cue, I reckoned, to head back.

We just about found our way but when we reached the huts the place had been transformed. There were even more people milling around, lots of them strangers to me, and at the centre of everything was a big open fire, like a bonfire. Balanced across its flames was a metal pole frame with pots dangling down. I saw Mum poking one of them. One sniff told me it was dinner. Other women were bring out plates and cutlery and the men were shifting boxes and crates and anything else they could find that might take a bum or two on top of it. Then we all sat down, round the fire, a cosy group of about forty people, and tucked in. I couldn't have been happier.

I like this hopping lark!

A lot of the men had bottles of stout and of course the night air was thick with cigarette smoke, but you didn't really notice it next to the bonfire. When we'd finished eating, the plates were stacked in a bucket – no one ever left any scraps – to be washed up in the morning.

With the combination of beer and people being away from home it didn't take long until a party broke out. There was singing, dancing and a lot of laughing. But it didn't seem to go on too late, not like the dos we had in London. But then, as Mum said as she dragged us in, in London we didn't all have to work in the morning. That was just the lucky ones like me . . .

When I went back into the hut it was transformed. We only had a little gas lamp to see by but I could tell Dad had laid the rug I'd ridden in over the floor so it felt warm under bare feet. And someone had done some extra work on the 'mattress', topping the edges off with clumps of bramble called faggots to give it some shape. We all got undressed, then climbed in. I didn't expect to sleep well at all on that bed of straw, what with it poking through the cover at various points, but a day of running and climbing had taken it out of me. I was asleep before the lamp was extinguished. From the sound of it, so was everyone else.

The last thing I remember was a mouse running over my cover.

'Hello, mouse,' I said, and that was it. Gone. Asleep. Too tired to even think.

I thought London was noisy. At least there were thick brick walls or floorboards in a flat between us and the neighbours. Tin, as it turned out, was not great for insulating against sound. As I lay in bed, trying to get my bearings on that first full day in the country, I could hear everything from next door, laughs, rows and, I swear, a big old fart from someone.

The noise, however, was even greater outside. When I looked out the window, I could see a right gathering on the common as horse and carts bounced their way over the uneven ground.

'What's going on?' I asked Mum.

'If we're lucky, it's our breakfast.'

She was right. With so many people packed into such a small area, the local baker had sent a cart out full of bread and cakes. If we weren't a captive audience I don't know who was. By the time he left the wagon was empty. The butcher did the same and so did the local dairy farm. By nine o'clock we had milk, which we stored in a bucket of water to keep cool, butter, meat and bread. All we were missing was a bit of fruit and veg. It wasn't long until a cart loaded with those supplies pulled up as well.

'About time,' Mum said.

I shrugged. I was happy with my toast and jam. There was no point getting shirty about carrots and spuds being late. But, I realised, there wasn't just groceries on the cart. There was a table, a dresser, all manner of pots and pans and two familiar-looking suitcases. It was only when I saw the big old brown cob harnessed at the front that I twigged.

'Tommy?'

I ran over to the cart and, sure enough, unclipping the panels round the back was Granddad. Tommy had carried our furniture all the way from Somers Town and, while he was at it, Granddad had decided to make a few bob selling some greenery.

As much as I wanted to hang around Granddad, Mum said it was time for us kids to go.

'Time to earn our keep,' she said, although she didn't look too happy about it. As we set off across the common I noticed all the other women and kids ahead of us, funnelling through the same gate I'd found exploring the day before. I told the others about the men on stilts I'd seen. Mum told me not to be silly but she had to laugh when we cleared the trees and there they were.

'Well, I never,' she said. 'I'll never doubt you again, Boy-Boy.'

One look at my happy face later and she added, 'On second thoughts, you can forget that.'

Mum was as much in the dark about what we were doing as us kids but she had the basic idea. Another woman showed us the ropes. We all grabbed a bushel basket from the nearby stack then took a seat on a crate near one of the large barrows I'd seen yesterday. They were full of hops still on their strings. Up close I could see the actual hop part on the vine was like a little lime-green acorn but instead of being smooth it was made of layers like a lady's petticoat or the petals on a rose. Our job, I was told, was to pick these little things from the vine and load them in the basket. The more hops you picked, the more you got paid.

I looked around. Kids outnumbered women. There was going to be some pretty money earned here. I wondered if I'd be allowed to keep any. Not that there was a sweet shop within sight.

The picking itself wasn't as easy as it looked. The first hop I tugged exploded into my palm. Inside it was full of yellow dust which was pretty but it went right up my nose. If these things smelled pungent from the side of the field, inhaling it was like having Vicks vapour spray inserted directly into your brain.

I didn't do that again.

I soon picked it up but, looking back, I'm surprised any of us could stay awake. Apart from making beer, hops was used as an ingredient in sedatives. I suppose if you were found sleeping on the job they could hardly blame you.

Like all kids, I found it fun at first, especially competing with my brother and sister. Wally and Marje, I noticed, were let off. When we stopped for lunch though, I was disappointed to have to eat sandwiches on my crate then get going again. By the end of the day I'd had enough of the smell to last me a lifetime.

My chores didn't stop there. Someone had already got the fire going and now we had our own pots to put on it. But yesterday's stuff was still dirty, so Dad sent me and Rosie over to the stand-pipe with an old pram frame and a bucket balanced inside – what else? – a Jaffa crate. I got a clip round the ear when we got back after half an hour, both soaked. It didn't stop us mucking around again the next time.

Granddad was staying the night, which was great news to us grandchildren. But, as the food was cleared away and the beers came out, it was the time of the adults to enjoy his company. Because while we were tidying up, he'd nipped inside the hut. When he came out it was in his full Pearly splendour. Obviously the family gave him a cheer. The others on our site, however, just gaped. Then one by one over they came to have a gawp and a laugh. Within an hour we had both sides of the common around our fire.

The day before I'd wanted to go back to London. Now London had come to me. I couldn't have been happier.

10

A Nice Bit of Stew

So, this was 'hopping'.

When Granddad returned home after his one night it felt like there was a bit of a gap in camp. Dad left it a couple of days then pulled on his own suit and told me to get mine out as well. There was no collecting to be done but just the sight of us two doing a little jig and a song and dance while one chap scraped at a washboard and Dad rattled his spoons lifted the whole hopping community. Because that's how we felt. We were our own little village miles from anywhere, it felt to me. I realised after a week that I hadn't thought of London for a couple of days.

At some point I thought to ask Mum when we'd be going home. 'Not for a few weeks yet,' she said. I know why I asked. Mum had a habit of springing it on us that we were moving house. I wanted a bit of warning if we were going to be leaving Kent, especially if I was going to be bundled up in a rug again. Aside from that, her answer didn't tell me much. The future, for a kid, doesn't have that much meaning. I couldn't picture that far ahead so I did what I always did and tried to have fun. I'd deal with tomorrow when it arrived.

Although we worked hard on the hop fields there were plenty of laughs, even when they were meant to be chores. One of the things Granddad brought down from home was our old tin bath. It took a few trips with the pram and a lot of balancing over the fire but eventually I got it filled up. Then the Dole kids were ordered in. Bathing in the kitchen at home was like a military operation. You were in and out, barely enough time to get wet, so there was enough warm water left for the whole family. In the summer air outside our hut it didn't matter what temperature the water was because you were hot anyway. It also didn't matter if you splashed a bit over the sides.

I say 'a bit'. The second Mum's back was turned there were soap-sud fights to the death. Imagine being shot by a pie gun in *Bugsy Malone*. That's what we looked like until the suds had all popped away. Then Mum would come over and moan about the mud puddle we'd made and out we'd get. Instead of a towel we'd just run around the common until we dried off. None of us had a care in the world.

Our first Sunday brought mixed emotions. It began well, with Mum lining up a roasting tray with a cut of beef from the butcher's weekend visit, some carrots and a load of spuds she'd peeled. I walked with her over to the farmer's cottage on the other side of the fields and watched as the farmer's wife somehow managed to squeeze the tray into her huge oven next to several other trays. Either she had a massive family or a lot of other hop-pickers had

had the same idea. An hour or so later I was despatched back over there, hopefully this time to pick up our roast dinner.

For a week I'd smelled only hops but the aromas as the farmer's wife opened her back door knocked me for six. Is there anything that smells as good as a roast? Not in my world. And there's nothing that tastes as good as a roast spud, either, is there?

The second I was out of the door I put the tray down and nicked a tater. It was delicious and crisp and the taste of beef dripping really made it melt on my tongue. Of course, it was piping hot so the second I bit in I got a mouthful of lava. But did that stop me? Twice more I had to stop to put that tray down. By the time I got back to the hut I was the most contented kid in the world – and I hadn't even had dinner yet.

That mood didn't last long. When Mum handed out the plates mine only had beef and carrots. I assumed the spuds must be coming but when I looked around everyone else had theirs already.

'Mum, where's me spuds?'

I'm not saying she sneered at me but it was a pretty mean laugh.

'You've eaten all yours,' she said. 'Don't tell me you didn't because I counted how many I peeled.'

'It was the farmer's wife!' I spluttered.

Whack.

I learned a lesson that day: never steal from a thief! They know all the tricks. The next Sunday, though, I did the same thing again. The spuds just seemed to taste better knowing I shouldn't be doing it.

The clip round the ear wasn't the worst thing about my first Sunday. After the pots had been cleaned – in water I'd collected – I saw Dad pulling on his boots.

'Can I come?' I asked him.

'You don't know where I'm going.'

'Where are you going?'

'Home. I've got work in the morning.'

Home? At the start of the week I would have bitten his hand off. Now, though, I wasn't sure I could even remember which street we currently lived on. As for the sounds and smells that I thought I couldn't live without, they seemed like a lifetime ago. No, I decided, I was staying put. I just wished Dad was, too.

'I'll be back Friday,' he promised. 'Be good. Keep 'em entertained, Prince Boy-Boy.'

Without Dad we had a bit more room in the hut but Mum found it harder and she wasn't afraid to pass her moods on to us. It suited her and me both if I kept out of her way when I wasn't hopping.

For most of the day, though, there we were either next to each other or opposite, shelling into the same basket. The only time I got off, apart from lunch, was when it was my turn to keep Wally and Marjie out of mischief. My way of doing that was to show them how to crush the hops which, of course, got us sent away pretty sharpish. The further we went, the harder it was for Mum to call us back. She didn't mind but Dave and Rosie made it clear how they felt missing out on their turns to mind the kids. Anything to get away from those bloomin' hops.

My dad wasn't the only fella to disappear on Sunday. Most of the dads were in the same boat so the whole site became a man-free zone. Nothing much really changed except that without a fifth of the population people started mixing together even more. Families took it in turns to cook for a strip of huts each meal. I didn't mind who cooked for me. I didn't even mind how they cooked. Or so I thought. One morning I watched a neighbour boil up her drawers and the family's smalls in a large pot over the fire. That night it was her turn to cook. As I sat down with my plate the woman said, 'Fancy a nice bit of stew, son?'

'Yes, please,' I replied.

But I went right off it when I saw she was using the same pot!

Even without the men, night-times were fun. Everyone still sat round the fire telling stories. When the wind picked up someone would come out with a couple of old sheets and tie them together around a stick and the nearest hut. It was classic make-do-and-mend. Then everyone would huddle together inside the windbreak area. It was a lovely time, just so nice and relaxed. I already knew then I would be coming back here all my life.

Come Friday night, though, and things changed again as gradually the menfolk started to turn up as each train from the old oak (*the Smoke, London*) came in. It was funny to watch, like a factory emptying for the day, as wave after wave of blokes with bags came marching through Bore Green Farm's gates.

Not all the dads were able to come back though, and there were more than a few wet eyes from those kids who didn't get to see their old man. But I was lucky. Working on a building site, even as hard as he did, had the advantage that the navvies liked to shut down early on a Friday and hit the beer houses. Dad might have had a couple but he also bought enough to take with him on the train. When he arrived he was carrying a whole crate of Toby light ale and a large cut of pork for our Sunday lunch. What more could a man want?

The men didn't just bring food and drink, however. The dynamic on the whole site changed over the weekend. Mostly for the good. Mostly.

After a couple of weeks going stir crazy, when Dad suggested we head off on the Saturday afternoon, the whole family went for it. The Elm Tree public house was back towards the station but, compared to the day we'd arrived, I was happy walking anywhere. When we arrived, en masse, there was already a fair amount of familiar faces catching the sun in the garden.

Dad bought us kids a lemonade each and threw a bag of crisps in our direction as well. After about a second's deliberation we then hightailed it for the woods. Even fizzy pop and crisps taste better when you're up a tree.

As the beer flowed at the Elm Tree – or the G&Ts, in Mum's case – spirits rose and strangers became friendly. Some became too friendly. Mum was always high-spirited, which is what Dad liked about her. Unfortunately other men liked it too. One fella in particular, a guy called Alvin, was getting a bit too friendly, cuddling up to Mum, giving her a squeeze when she made a joke. I don't think it bothered her but Dad didn't like it.

'Oi, Alvin,' he said, 'keep your distance or I'll have to find your missus.'

A bit later he lifted Alvin's arm off Mum's neck and put it on his mate's, along with another friendly warning. Whatever he did, Dad tried to keep the mood playful. But Alvin was a bit too far gone. Eventually his hand strayed somewhere it shouldn't and Mum pushed him away.

'Leave off, Alvin,' she said. 'I'm not interested.'

Alvin didn't budge, which was his last mistake. Dad was over him in a flash and gave him an uppercut right in the ribs. Alvin went down like a sack of spuds. I'll never forget the look of surprise on his face. It never left him until he started coughing and spluttering.

Dave and I didn't know whether to laugh or cheer. Our Dad had just lamped someone for being unnecessary with his lady. This was the stuff of knights of old. Dad was a hero!

He didn't see it like that, you could tell. Straight after the punch he picked up his pint and said to whoever was listening, 'I told him to leave well alone and he wouldn't listen. I told him. I gave him fair warning.' On and on he went, beating himself up until one of Alvin's brothers came over.

'He was asking for it, Alf, don't you worry. I would have chinned him myself if you hadn't.'

Alvin didn't see it quite like that. He yelled all sorts at Dad when he got up but as soon as Dad looked at him the fella legged it. He went home that Sunday and never came back.

Everyone else soon got back to their drinks and their laughing but every time I looked at Dad I could see he was troubled by what he'd done, which was a shame, because Dave and me spent the rest of our night re-enacting it.

*

Shook up though he was by his altercation with Alvin, it wasn't the last time I saw Dad use his fists that weekend. It turned out that Mum was terrified of mice. While I used to lie awake at night and watch the tiny little critters burrow around at the foot of our mattress, she'd sleep through it. That night, though, she must have been late to bed because I was awoken by her screaming. We all were.

If you think women standing on chairs when they see a mouse is something made up by cartoons, you're wrong.

'There it is, there it is!' she was shouting.

'Turn it down, Mary, you'll wake the whole common up.'

'It's too late for that!' came a voice from the other side of the tin wall.

Dad swore and struggled out of the low bed, already reaching for his boot. As soon as he was upright Mum screamed again and pointed to the little rodent skittling along the edge of the room. A second later it froze as Dad's boot fizzed past it and crashed against the wall, sending echoes all around us and causing more shouts from our neighbours.

Dad swore again and, as he lumbered towards the mouse, it dived into a hole in the floor.

The thing about mice, Dad said, is they never go in a hole without having an exit.

'There must be another hole nearby,' he shouted. 'Find it and block it.'

I saw a tiny space in the corner. It looked too small for my finger let alone an animal.

'That's it!' Dad said. 'Stuff your sock in it. Now!'

I did as I was told. Meanwhile Dad told us all to be quiet and he got himself comfortable on his knees above the other hole, one arm raised in the air behind him.

I don't know how long passed but the neighbours settled down. Mum had stopped shaking although she hadn't taken her eyes off the hole. Neither had Dad. I didn't know what he was planning but I couldn't sleep until it was over.

I didn't have to wait too long. At first there was a scratching sound, then I saw a flicker of movement at the mouth of the hole. Then a tiny creature popped out.

The last thing it would have seen was a shadow in the moonlight. Dad's fist came down at such speed the mouse stood no chance. The noise once again drew complaints from next door, but not as much as Dad's cursing did. He wasn't swearing about the mess of blood and fur on his knuckles or the pain that must have been coursing through him now the adrenaline was wearing off. All he cared about was the fact that he'd smashed so hard the front of his signet ring had exploded on impact.

'Bloody mice,' he said.

Now it was Mum's turn to think he was a hero. But she still made him clear up the mess.

A few days later we got some new visitors that Mum wasn't scared of. Granddad and Grandma came down by train to spend the week. I asked him why he didn't bring Tommy.

'Because we wanted to get here in a hurry,' he explained. Uncle Patsy, he said, was looking after the shop and the stables.

Somehow they squeezed into our hut. With Dad gone again it

was just about doable but I woke up with Rosie or Wally on top of me most mornings.

Granddad brightened up the evenings but he was also a dynamo in the hopping fields. When he arrived the forecast was rain so he'd brought two large umbrellas – like golfing umbrellas we have today. With the sun shining that morning, he said, 'If you can fill this umbrella with hops, Uncle Bill will take you swimming.'

'You're on.'

Because there were two brollies it became a competition between me and my sister. When she won I wasn't happy.

'Best of three,' I said.

'If you want.'

So off we went again and again until I won or got fed up trying. All the while Granddad was stifling his laugh. Not only had he tricked us into doing his share of the hopping, we were doing it in double-quick time.

Maybe there was a reason I put off finishing though, because when we finally caught up with Uncle Bill at the lake I realised I was nervous.

'Seven years old and you can't swim? Come here, Alfie, and I'll teach you.'

With that he grabbed hold of me under the arms and flung me into the lake. I was already screaming when I hit the water. If I hadn't, I might have panicked and sucked in a mouthful. As it was, as soon as my feet hit the bottom of the lake I pushed up as hard as I could.

And found myself standing in thigh-high water.

On the side, Uncle Bill was laughing as he stripped down to his shorts.

'Lesson one,' he called out. 'Always know how deep the water is before you jump in.'

'But I didn't jump,' I shouted as I waded out. 'You pushed me.'

'No, I didn't,' he said – and threw me in again.

By the early evening my sister and brothers and I could all keep ourselves pretty much afloat. Even Wally. By the time Granddad and Grandma left at the weekend we could all swim. I couldn't believe how fantastic it felt, suspended one minute, powering along under your own steam the next. And what's better than swimming? Jumping in. When the banks of the lake got too timid we started leaping off the side of the river. That had the advantage of a downhill current, so double the fun. Or double the danger, depending on how you viewed it. For kids they're both the same.

I got more than one clip round the ear for swimming when I should have been working or eating or doing something else. But at least Mum knew where to find me.

Swimming wasn't the only thing Uncle Bill taught us. When he suggested fishing I shook my head.

'It sounds boring.'

David and Rosie agreed.

'It's not boring,' Uncle Bill laughed. 'It's a skill. Maybe you're too scared you won't be able to do it?'

You could tell I was my father's son. A challenge or a dare to me is like a silver-foil bottle top to a magpie.

'I'll show you,' I said, although I had no clue what I was going to show anyone.

David and Rosie had seen enough. 'We'll leave you to have "fun",' Dave said sarcastically. 'Hop picking is better than this.'

For all my love of swimming and its messy, hectic, boisterous energy, the second Uncle Bill put a rod in my hands I realised I had a stillness inside me that I hadn't noticed. I was always haring around, running from this place to that place. I never read a book, I didn't get on at school and I hated not being on the go. But with a stick in my hand I discovered I could sit still all day.

And that's what it was: a stick. My uncle snapped off a branch from a willow, pulled all the small bits off then, when we had a length of about three feet, he tied some string around one end. At the other end of the string he tied a bit of left-over cooking fat.

'Now,' he said, 'watch this.'

He lowered the fat into the river and – nothing happened. A minute passed, two minutes, three minutes. After about five, he pulled the string out. The fat was gone.

'See, there's something in there,' he said.

I thought about what it could be. I'd been swimming in that river!

Then Bill got a little hook out of his pocket and tied that to the string. This time he shoved another piece of fat onto the hook.

'This'll keep 'em busy,' he said, grinning, then lowered the string back in. This time he gave me the stick to hold.

'Tell me when it starts moving,' he instructed, and lay back on the bank to catch forty winks.

'How will I know?'

At that second I felt the string tug the end of the stick. Bill saw it and sat bolt upright next to me.

'Easy, Boy-Boy! Just hold the rod firm for a moment till . . . Now, lift it!'

I pulled on the stick and I was surprised at how heavy it was. Bill leaned over and helped me out. When the end of the string came out there was no sign of the fat or the hook. All we could see was a surprised-looking silver fish.

'Good work, Boy-Boy. That's a nice-looking perch.'

It wasn't just the fish that was hooked – so was I. I thought swimming was the best thing in the world but that was just fun. This was more like a sport. And, I discovered that night, you got to eat your winnings. After that, any day I didn't come home with half a dozen fish for dinner Mum was disappointed. On the plus side, having fish to cook was more valuable to the family than hop picking so Mum excused me – 'On condition you bring us back a beauty.'

I was happy to, but the best thing about it was the look on Dave's face.

'Still worse than hop picking, is it?' I called out as I left the hut. I just got outside before his shoe flew past my ear.

Happy days.

By the time we'd been in Kent four weeks I'd forgotten any other life. But things had to change. In our family they always did. When Mum announced that the hopping season was over – all the hops were stripped from the binds – my heart sank and I prepared myself for another move. One where I couldn't swim and fish all day. But that wasn't what she meant. The hops might all be picked but there were fourteen acres of potatoes that needed digging out of the ground – and she'd signed us up for that.

The first clue about how hard this would be was when I saw all the carts being dragged onto the common. One by one the huts on our strip were emptied – pots, pans, tables, chairs, food, suitcases and, finally, people were all piled on board. By the end of the weekend it was like a ghost town.

'Afraid of hard work, they are,' Mum sniffed.

I'm not sure she knew what she was letting us in for. I'd never picked a field of potatoes before and neither had she. Clearly the lot who left had done because it was backbreaking work, even for someone close to the ground like me. By the end of day one I was too tired even to swim but because I was filthy with mud I forced myself. That was preferable to lugging the water pram over the common and back half a dozen times to fill the tin bath.

With all the remaining grown-ups busy with the Maris Pipers, that left the hop-picking area empty. In particular, the huge bins where the hops were stored were ripe for hiding in. Better yet, we could throw Wal in and he'd be too small to climb out. When he complained to Mum we denied it, as you do. One sniff of his clothes and face and hands – and even backside; these hops get everywhere – told its own tale.

We finished the potatoes just before the weather turned for the worse. With the start of October our summer adventure was well and truly over. When Mum said things were changing again, this time she meant it. We spent all of one morning packing everything up and all around us I could see the remaining families doing the same. It was only when Mum told me to take the rug outside and beat it I remembered how I'd travelled down.

'I'm not going back inside this am I, Mum?' I asked. 'It's filthy.'

'No, love, I promise you you're not.'

By lunchtime everything was boxed and stacked on the common. There were already three or four carts there when I heard a horn toot and saw a large flatbed lorry swing into the field. The rains had made the common slippery but somehow it got over to our row. In the front seat I could see Granddad's beaming smile.

'I thought you'd like to ride back in style,' he called out the window.

'Anything's better than being wrapped in a carpet,' I said.

An hour later I wasn't so sure. There were three other families and us crammed onto the back of the truck along with all our furniture and luggage. For a roof we had a canvas tarpaulin that might just as well have not been there. As the rains plummeted down I thought I was going to drown.

But, as the view that I hadn't been allowed to see on the way to Paddock Wood blended gradually into the familiar sight of terraced houses and grey, smoky streets, I realised I wasn't happy. Fishing and swimming were my life now. What did London have to offer me after that?

11

Come In, Number Six

We'd moved again. While we were away Dad had upped sticks and shifted us all round the corner to Werrington Street. It was a weird place, flagstone floors throughout, like a castle, but even though it was big – ten times the size of our hut in Kent – I still felt like I'd had my wings clipped coming back. It was because the hut was so small that we spent so much time sitting outside. Eating in the kitchen now, a couple of feet from where Mum was cooking, made me a bit anxious. Claustrophobic, even. I longed for the open spaces.

'If you're good we'll go again next year,' Mum said.

I'd never made a promise to God before but I did then. I would be as good as gold, I told Him, if He'd let us go back to the hopping huts next summer.

Religion wasn't a big part of my family. Grandma sometimes took us to Christmas mass at the church on Phoenix Road but apart from weddings, christenings and funerals, that was the sum total of our link with Jesus. Out of the blue, when we moved, Mum decided it was time to do more.

'I think we might be Catholic,' she said one day. 'You should go to a Catholic school.'

That was it. Instant overnight conversion.

I don't know if she told anyone or just dumped us at the new place. All I knew is, one day I went to Netley's and the next I was at St Aloysius on Aldenham Street, surrounded by priests and statues. And it really was the next day, too. David's feet were just too big to share boots with. Mum had had to give in and buy me my own pair.

Thinking about it now, I'm not sure how much religion was the driving force, really. Netley's was all the way over the other side of the Hampstead Road, tucked between Stanhope Street and William Road, whereas you could virtually see St Aloysius from the front room of our new place in Werrington Street. If you were pegging washing out in the back yard at lunchtime you could certainly hear it, as Mum was quick to remind me every afternoon. Still, for convenience alone, I think St Aloysius could have been a Jewish school and Mum would still have found a way to get us in.

It wasn't just for the sake of our legs that she wanted us close to home. About once a month she got a note from the head-master at Netley's asking her and Dad to come in to talk about my behaviour. Dad went once but never again. Mum trotted over on her own usually but mainly it was just for show. Whatever the head said I'd done – not turned up, pinched this, cheeked this teacher – Mum wouldn't hear. She'd just switch off, waiting until she could get me outside for a wallop. Then she'd drag me by the ear back home, or as far as she could keep her grip before I wriggled free. Usually I'd be the other side of the Hampstead Road with the sound of her shouting following me closer than she did.

The switch itself didn't make much difference to me. Both schools were big, yellow Victorian cathedrals. It didn't matter how big you were, walking into the playground at St Aloysius for the first time was daunting. It was like being in a castle. An unfriendly castle or, worse, a prison. You could empty Wormwood Scrubs into the place and the inmates wouldn't notice the difference.

As for the kids, I knew just as many in my new school because it was local. Even the kids who weren't Catholic found it easy to pretend. You just needed to know a few saints' names and do as you were told. The saints bit I could do in my sleep. Doing as I was told . . . Well, put it this way: Mum still got to stretch her legs once in a while to come and visit.

The problem was the priests. We didn't see eye to eye on almost anything, but especially not the big things. They were hot on attendance, punctuality, uniform, homework, manners, cleanliness, obedience – none of them my *Mastermind* specialist subjects, exactly.

They were mean with it too. Whacks with rulers, a bit of hair pulling I could put up with. Having a balding, fat man with halitosis screaming at me that I was going to burn in hell if I didn't finish my times tables was actually terrifying for a seven-year-old. Mum gave it until Christmas then yanked me out. The primary on Polygon Road had a place, and what's more it was C of E.

Alf's Grandfather George Dole at Epsom Derby, early 1900s
with his daughter Annie

George Dole appearing on *This Is Your Life* with Eamonn Andrews in
1964. Bert Matthews in pearls on left

A young Alf, in the early 1950s

Alf's mum, Mary, with Alf's sister and brother, Pauline and Peter, 1940s

Alf (far left) with Wally (third from left in front) and other hopping friends, mid-1950s

Mother Mary, Alf, Wally and Alf Senior, hopping, mid-1950s

Peter, Pauline, Alf Senior, Mary and their granddaughter at work in the hopping fields, 1950s

Alf and Wally with their two aunties, Polly and Annie, in foreground, at left

Hopping in the 1950s

Alf Senior and Mary in their hopping hut, 1950s

Alf and his motor car, hopping common, 1950s

(From left) Brother David, Alf Senior, Mary, sisters Rosie and Pauline, Brother Wally and Alf having a good time in the 1950s

Alf, Mary, his third partner, and cousin (blonde hair) outside hopping hut, 1980s

Presenting a cheque to Great Ormond Street Hospital, 1988. Alf on the right playing the spoons

Alf and his daughter Diane, Pearly Princess of St Pancras, at The Merrie Harriers pub in Cowbeech at their 'dig for victory' show, 2007

Alf and Diane in the Pearly Cab

Alf and Boris Johnson, St George's Day, Leadenhall Market, 2009

Alf playing the spoons

Fundraising with
the Pearly Cab

'A proper religion,' as Mum called it – although not within earshot of Grandma. She wasn't daft.

There was a reason that Mum didn't like a long walk any more. By the time I was eight I had another brother on the way. I didn't know the ins and outs – as it were – of sex back then but if anyone had been trying for a baby in the hopping huts I think the whole row would have known.

It didn't matter where we moved to, people always knew where to find us. I was at home one day when there was a hammering on the door, then it flew open – it was never locked if we were in. When it slammed shut I saw the McCann boys, two Irish brothers who lived near where we used to on Charrington Street.

'Mary, love, the Old Bill's on our case – can we hide up here a while?'

Mum barely flinched. I wondered how often this sort of thing happened while I was at school.

'Sit yourselves down and I'll get you a cuppa.'

'Thanks, Mary, you're an angel.'

'Don't be soft,' she laughed. 'But I've got to keep the bookies on my side, haven't I?'

Now they all laughed. I was none the wiser but I discovered the McCanns were runners for a bookmaker on Camden High Street. Gambling was legal but collecting bets out and about was not. Somers Town was a pretty small patch really and there wasn't a copper who didn't know the McCanns' faces. The second they were spotted going into a house that wasn't theirs, the whistles blew. They'd been doing some business on Aldenham Street when the police spoiled their fun.

'I wasn't sure which number you were,' one of them admitted.

'Well, don't get too used to it. You never know how long we'll be here.'

That wasn't what I wanted to hear. *Ah well . . .*

Like Granddad, Uncle Patsy and just about every other grown-up, Mum and Dad liked a bet. Horses usually, sometimes greyhounds, and pigeons whenever anything was flying in Dole colours. Aunt Annie actually married a bookie. Horseracing was his speciality although he'd take your pound on two woodlice rolling on a table if you asked him. I never met a poor book-maker – still haven't – and whenever he turned up you knew it wouldn't be long before Mum unlocked the front room, because he never arrived empty-handed. A crate of bottles wouldn't be far from him – and they didn't contain lemonade.

The days of shinning up oak trees and splashing around in the lake seemed to be so long ago I sometimes wondered if I'd dreamed it all. Being told to have a bath in winter sent me run-ning out the front door. The idea of diving in an open-air pond seemed crazy.

Heat was a problem. Although there were fireplaces in most of the rooms, the only one that really got stoked up was in the main room with the kitchen in. We'd all huddle round that but getting firewood wasn't easy. Coal was expensive and there wasn't a farmer on a tractor dropping off a delivery of faggots once a week. There weren't even any trees we could lop down. We were going to freeze if Dad didn't do something, but without work – the building sites shut down in winter and decorating wasn't much better – buying fuel was out of the question.

'We'll be burning the chairs if I don't get some pay soon,' he said one day, and I still don't know if he was joking.

Then inspiration hit. He came running in one night and told me to follow him to Granddad's.

'What for?'

'We need his barrow.'

Fifteen minutes later we were outside the goods depot on Ossulston Street. Now all the building work on the flats opposite was done, the council were repairing the roads, laying lots of new tarry bricks. These were blocks of wood covered in tar laid down together like a jigsaw or a stretch of parquet flooring to form a surface fit for traffic. Because of the way they were made, they also absorbed any old crap that was lying around when they were shipped and, obviously, each piece had its own bit of London embedded in the top. Some were more worse for wear than others. That's why the road was being relaid.

So what were the navvies doing with the old ones? Nothing, once we arrived. It took us half an hour but soon we had a tower of black filthy road balancing on the barrow. Dad was pleased as punch.

'This should keep us burning till summer!'

By the time we got back home and had unloaded it all into the yard, Dad's confidence had waned.

'We need more,' he said quietly. 'Let's go back.'

It was ten o'clock by now and freezing. I had two scarves and a pair of David's old gloves missing a fingertip on each hand. The last thing I wanted to be doing was peeling nasty, tarry wood off a scrapheap in sub-zero temperatures. It turned out that I was in the minority. As we turned into Ossulston Street you'd have thought it was market day. The road was jammed with carts and barrows and masses of men who'd either had the same idea as Dad or had seen what we'd been up to.

'Come on, Boy-Boy, we'll need to be sharp!'

Suddenly all my tiredness vanished. Yes, we were doing the same disgusting job, but this time it was a competition! I had people to beat. Now there was something to play for.

There were enough kids my age there dragged out of bed to help out. Those were the ones I managed to nick a few blocks from. I also managed to sniff out the bigger pieces for Dad to come over and drag back, rather than have us shift three or four bits in as many trips. I don't know whether we won any prizes but when Dad called time I was actually disappointed. But then I thought of actually burning one of these things and I couldn't wait to get back.

Only Mum was up when we got back. The hearth was still glowing so after I warmed myself up I headed upstairs to bed.

'Don't you want to see what one of these burns like?' Dad called out.

Exhaustion nearly won but my curiosity got the better of me.

'Yes!' I said, and bounded back into the room.

Dad went into the yard and came back with a piece of 'tarry' about a foot square.

'This should do us,' he said, and tossed it onto the centre of the orange dust.

At first nothing happened. Then there was a bit of hissing and we all watched the tar begin to melt. Suddenly there was a crack behind me and a mirror smashed to floor.

'What?'

Before anyone could react another mini-explosion happened by Dad's feet. In no time we were up and all standing out of reach of the fireplace. What the hell was going on?

'It's the tar,' Dad said resignedly. 'After all those years being trampled on it's embedded with stones and glass and all sorts.'

As he spoke we saw another missile fly out of the flames.

'Alfred Dole,' Mum said, 'what have you brought into our house?'

'I don't know,' he said; but, as a vase on the dresser pinged off its shelf, he laughed. 'It's fun though, isn't it?'

The next morning Dad fitted a mesh guard around the hearth. Any more friendly fire should be stopped before it left the brick-work, he reckoned. He was right but, even if he wasn't, the heat a single tarry block chucked out was worth the odd bruise from a flying pebble. I didn't know about reaching summer but we'd certainly not be freezing downstairs for a while.

That was, if we reached summer. The missiles might have stayed in the fireplace but the smoke the blocks chucked out was horrendous. Even for a kid raised in the smoky atmosphere of No. 151's back room, the smog coming out of the fire smelled like a poisonous cloud. After a while Dad even opened a window, but

Mum quickly shut it again. We'd have to put up with the fumes if we wanted to keep warm.

It turned out that the smog and stones were the least of our troubles. There's a reason things like tar aren't sold for fuel. If a bit gets blown up the chimney and decides to stick to the wall, you've got a problem. Luckily the tar wasn't too far up so we could actually see the flames licking back down the chimney flue.

'Christ, Mary,' Dad said, 'fetch us some salt, will you!'

While Mum went one way Dad dived the other, coming back with a pan of water. It couldn't have been a big piece of tar because he managed to extinguish the mini-blaze in one slosh of the pan – and without completely dousing the main fire below.

'Here's your salt, Alf,' Mum said, handing over the table cellar. 'What on earth do you want it for?'

'We'll have to line the chimney with it, stop it burning up again. Tar won't burn salt.'

'If you say so.'

'I do. Although I think we'll be needing a bit more than this.'

It turns out we were lucky. The fire brigade was called out in Somers Town at least three times that I saw due to burning chimneys. Luckily the trucks weren't far, opposite Euston Station. But one family lost its home and a couple of people went to hospital.

Did it stop anyone using the tarry blocks, though?

Not on your nelly. If we could have afforded coal, that would have been different. But needs must and if it meant risking your family's life to keep warm, so be it. That's just the way it had to be.

*

Somehow we got through winter without any loss of life. Spring brought its own near fatality, however. Marjorie had got a cat and of course it liked sleeping on her bed. When the warmer weather came, it decided to sit on the window ledge. I thought cats were meant to be intelligent. This one couldn't tell if the window was open or shut. It was, even at the time, an old sash window and so when it opened it could go three or four foot high. Us kids knew not to muck around near it because we were on the second floor. The cat didn't worry about things like that. Whether he was just trying to lean against the glass or what, I don't know. But I happened to be outside, coming home, when I saw it falling out, spinning.

I wonder sometimes if the creator of Wile E. Coyote was watching that day because that cat did everything a cartoon character does when it realises it's not on terra firma any more. It flapped, it span, it tried to run, all in the space of one or two seconds.

And then the inevitable happened: it landed on all fours, licked its bollocks, and walked away without even a limp.

What did you expect? It's a cat, after all. Although I reckon it was down a couple of lives after that.

The warm weather seemed to put Mum in a good mood, too. Maybe she just couldn't be bothered keeping tabs on us, but when I asked to go exploring in Regent's Park she just said, 'Be back for your tea.'

Great, I thought. *Freedom to roam!*

I didn't have a clue what to do there although having a chat with whatever animals at the zoo were nearest the railings was top of my list. That was before I found the canal. It wasn't clean but that hadn't stopped loads of kids jumping in between the locks at Camden. All along the towpath there were little piles of shorts and vests. Everyone was in their pants, even the younger girls. It took as long as I needed to reach them before I was in there as well.

Every so often we'd all have to get out when a boat came along. The basin was wide enough for it to pass but the horse towing it on the path would trample all our clothes if we didn't shift them. Sometimes one of the newer diesel barges came chugging through with its front stacked to the brim with coal or bricks or whatever it was transporting. We didn't move for those, however loud the driver shouted. Nobody thought about propeller accidents then.

Nobody thought about lots of things. The top of the canal was like dishwater after a roast, covered in a deep, sticky film. Fat in your sink at home is one thing, though, because that only reaches your wrists. We were swimming in the stuff. God knows how much spilled oil or diesel I swallowed. It didn't taste too bad so we just ignored it.

Swimming between the locks had another danger. You could only stay in the basin if the narrow boat was coming 'downhill' towards you, that is, travelling east from Camden to King's Cross with you on the King's Cross side. When the sluice gates on the lock opened there was an almighty wave as 150 tons of water came pouring out. Those were the golden times. That's when we could pretend we were at sea.

That was the fun part. Anyone in the high part of the water

near a gate when a boat was stepping down was asking for trouble. As soon as those gates open deep below the surface, the water rushes through at a dangerous rate, like a whirlpool, and anyone too close could get swept along in the current. If you were lucky, you'd be small enough to get sucked through the sluice gates and spat out the other side. If you were too big to fit through you'd either get stuck halfway and drown or, worse, the boat driver would lower the paddles and you'd get guillotined. Either way, your swimming days would be over and the lock wouldn't be much use to the tradesmen for a while.

When the locks started getting busy I got out. After all, it was Regent's Park I'd come to see. Still dripping, I padded my way along the towpath towards the zoo. On my way, though, I saw an animal I didn't expect.

I was just heading round the bend towards the old Pickfords shed goods depot when I heard shouting. Proper shouting. Men giving orders and women screaming. Obviously I put my head down and ran as fast as my bare feet would allow.

I eventually found a crowd and forced my way through the legs. In the water there was a horse looking as terrified as I could imagine. It turned out he'd been towing a boat and got startled by a train thundering by. He wasn't the first and he wouldn't be the last, but I didn't know that. I could not see any way how the horse was going to get out until I saw a guy stripped to waist and jumping in. He swam out to the horse and managed to throw a rope around its neck. Then he got out of the way sharpish while four lads on the bank started to pull. Eventually they got the horse over to below where they were standing, where there happened to be a ramp leading out. Horses fell in so often round here, the council had put that in place. If it happened anywhere else the horse was in trouble.

I realised I'd spent so much time wandering that it had to be nearly time to head back and I hadn't even reached the park. All the industry and excitement along the towpath was too fascinating. But I had to go. I didn't want to be banned next time.

Over the next few days I not only watched the industry, I managed to blag a few rides on the back of a boat and I got to walk a horse – although not near the train track. I also discovered a new swimming place that was worth its weight in gold.

On the bend as the canal pulls away from Camden you've got a bridge linking Primrose Hill to the zoo entrance at Regent's Park. I was walking towards it one day when I saw a kid throw something into the water. At first I thought it was a stone but then I saw his brother ask his dad for something, then he threw that. It glistened in the sunlight on the way down then the dad said, 'I hope you made a wish.' That was no stone.

It's money. They're throwing money away!

I could not believe what I was seeing. Of course, you see it with fountains everywhere. People love to throw money into water. But in that day and age, when families like mine were literally nicking road scraps to heat our houses? It seemed all wrong to me. *But*, I thought, *if they don't want it, I know a kid who does.*

I stripped down and jumped into the water when no one was overhead. I didn't want to put off any more donors. Then I swam out to the middle and dived down. The canal wasn't deep – only about five feet – but upside down it felt like I'd paddled a mile. I felt my hand hit the sludge on the bottom and immediately realised what a terrible idea this was. I span round and pushed off the bottom with my feet. As I did, I felt something between my toes.

Damn it. That was a coin!

I tried to propel myself down again but it was too late, the current had moved me. But at least I knew something was there if I had the patience.

It took me a while but I found a pocketful of change before the afternoon was out. When I showed Mum she couldn't have been happier – because she took them off me and said, 'That'll pay for your dinner tonight.'

That's the last time I show you my winnings . . .

When I wasn't metal detecting there were other places along the water that had their own different lures. The old fizzy pop manufacturer, Idris & Co. (before it was consumed by Britvic), had its original factory in Pratt Street. At certain points of the day, however, a truck would tip the company's carbonated waste into the canal at the foot of Arlington Street. It sounds stupid but that was the time to be in the water. I didn't know what they were pumping but it was so warm. However sunny the day, you can't have water hot enough to swim in.

Of course, there was no health and safety in 1938, or none that I was aware of, and for all I know I was doing my best breaststroke in chemicals and hazardous waste. But the whole place smelled wonderful for a few minutes, even if it didn't taste so good.

Further round the canal, towards Little Venice, there was a nice, uninterrupted long stretch. That, I decided, was the place to dangle a line. I went up there with a pot of food scraps and fat one day and never looked back. Perch and roach, the odd carp and a load of pike all came out. And cuttlefish as well. I'd never seen one before I watched an old boy fill a bucket just by dipping a line down to the bed. It was shellfish for dinner that night, once we'd worked out what to do with them.

Fishing, though, didn't stop at the canal. Eventually I got as far as the park and, once I'd worn myself out diving for farthings, I decided to treat myself to an ice cream from the little booth, followed by a boat ride up in the pond at the north side. Most kids had a grown-up with them but I just had my ice cream and the correct change. It was only a rowing boat – how hard could it be?

It was all about rhythm and coordination, both of which I seemed to have left in the canal. But eventually I got the hang of it and, while the guy renting out the boats laughed at me, I managed to steer my way towards the centre of the lake and round behind a little island. That's when the idea struck. Why waste being out of sight of grown-ups?

My ice cream wasn't the only thing I'd boarded with. In my pocket I had my trusty fishing line, a hook and some scraps of fat. I threw the line over the side of the boat and lay back, feet up, waiting for the familiar tug.

It didn't take long. I was actually giggling to myself as I wound the perch in. It was a beauty. We would dine well that night.

Unfortunately, I wasn't the only person who saw it. While I'd been lying down the boat had drifted back round the island into the view of the owner.

'Oi,' he bellowed. 'Come in, number six, your time is up. And throw that sodding fish back!'

To hell with that. I dug the oar into the bottom of the lake and pushed with all my might. Two more goes like that and I'd punted to the opposite edge of the pond. Then, grabbing my fish, I was out and over the fence while the boat fella was still running round the side.

I didn't think my summer could get any better, but I'd forgotten about hopping. If anything, that year's trip to Paddock Wood was even better. I saw a few family members I hadn't seen all year and met up with some friends who'd been in our row of huts. The occasional visits from the menfolk, especially Dad and Granddad, were again highlights. Best of all, I had my own seat in the train on the way down – and Wally was stuffed on the luggage rack. Tommy, once again, arrived the next day with our furniture, luggage and a load of produce from No. 151.

It was another blissful month and a half of hopping, fishing and swimming until Granddad arrived, again on Tommy, to collect everything up. This time we all caught the train back, although I begged to go along with Granddad in the cart. I'm actually glad he said 'no'.

I didn't see Granddad get home later that day and when I bumped into him in the shop I could tell something was wrong.

'What is it?' I asked him.

'It's Tommy,' he said. 'He didn't make the journey home.'

I burst into tears right there. Tommy and Kitty, even that silly goat, Billy, meant as much to me as a lot of my friends. It was worse knowing that the poor old horse had died carrying my stuff back. But, as Dad pointed out later, it's pretty much all uphill on the way back from Kent and Tommy wasn't young.

Apparently he'd just stopped going up one road, gave a little whinny, then keeled over, snapping his reins as he went down. Granddad admitted he had cried for an hour as he watched his precious horse just give up the fight. Then he had to dust himself down and walk miles to find help. Not only did he have all our furniture to look after, he needed help shifting Tommy.

I thought I would never enjoy the hopping season again after that but, as the following summer came round and we picked up our letters from Dr Shaw, I knew I couldn't wait to get back down there. Excitement outweighed guilt – which made me feel even worse. Dad saw it. He could be so quiet and thoughtful sometimes but it always surprised me when he was.

'It's not your fault Tommy died, Boy-Boy,' he said. 'Don't let anything like that ruin your holiday.'

'I won't, Dad, I promise. I'll never let anything ruin my hopping holidays again.'

Then, two weeks later, I had a half-full umbrella by my side when a hysterical woman came running into the field.

'We're all going to die!' she screamed. 'Hitler's on his way!'

12

They're Taking You Away

Everything changed. And nothing.

One day we weren't 'at war' with Germany. The next day we were. It seemed very sudden to me. The grown-ups might have been expecting it but I didn't read newspapers and most adults kept their conversations light in front of kids. It didn't help that I had no clue where Germany was and I'd never heard of Hitler either. The Great War wasn't on our school syllabus. Either that or it had been taught on one of my days off.

But there was an effect, of sorts. No work got done at Bore Green Farm for a couple of days but nothing bad happened either. In fact, nothing much happened at all. People gossiped and argued and made predictions about the end of the world or the 'Empire' getting bigger. Some people thought the war was a good thing, most thought it was bad. The men, in particular, seemed rocked by it. That was when I first heard the word 'conscription'.

Apparently the first hints of combat were given earlier in the year when the government put all young men aged between twenty and twenty-two on alert that they might be called up into the army as 'militia men'. By the time the Prime Minister, Mr Chamberlain, declared we were at war, everyone suspected that it wouldn't be long before more mature heads and bodies were summoned. That's what had happened during the Great War. No one knew, just yet, what that age limit would be. Granddad, we assumed, would be safe. He was old and his shop was an essential part of the community. Dad, though, was born in September 1901. Would the forces take men as old as him?

They did back in 1916.

If Dad was worried about it he put on a brave face. Mum was less concerned about appearances. She mentioned again and again to anyone who had the time to listen all the stress Dad had suffered carrying the hot cement. He was in no state, mentally or physically, she insisted, to be training with young men. He certainly couldn't be expected to go into battle.

Dad kept trying to assure her.

'They'll not sign me up, love. I'm nearly forty. There's a lot of stronger and younger men than me.'

But it wasn't long before news trickled through to Paddock Wood. We all stood round the fire one morning after breakfast while one fella read out that day's headlines.

'They're doing it,' he said. 'All men between eighteen and forty-one are liable to be called up.'

He looked around at all the faces listening. We all immediately thought of David back home. He was fifteen and old enough to be working on the markets. In three years he'd be old enough to pick up a rifle. Even those fellas who were outside the age limit looked sad. The last war was so fresh for the grown-ups there was no getting away from what a call-up could mean.

Dad refused to buckle. 'You'll not get rid of me that easily,' he said. 'I'm no good to them. I've got no skills.'

'Less of the stiff upper lip, Alfie, or they'll definitely sign you up,' Mum laughed. Then, in seriousness, she suggested, 'Maybe you could get yourself a job down a mine? They're exempt.'

'Where are there mines near us, woman?' he laughed.

'I don't know. But we could move.'

The very idea made me feel sick. But if it kept Dad with us . . .

'No, let's just trust in common sense. The odds of me being picked at my age aren't worth worrying about. No one's going to put me in charge of a submarine.'

Things might not have changed much in Kent, but coming back to Somers Town in Granddad's rented lorry I soon noticed that things weren't right. The first thing I spotted was that all the houses in Werrington Street looked like they'd been abandoned. The ones with wooden shutters had them closed, even in day-light, and the ones without had nailed planks of two-by-four over the windows or large sheets of cardboard inside.

'What's going on, Granddad?'

'It's the blackout, son. We can't have Hitler seeing where we are.'

Nine years old and being asked to imagine that some person would send aeroplanes over at night-time to bomb our houses? It did not compute, not for me.

'Why would they do that?'

'They want our land,' Granddad said. 'But we're not going to let them have it.'

What good is our land if it's all bombed up? I wondered. But that and other questions could be answered later. We had to unload our gear, and then get started on our own windows. Once again, the familiar pile of Jaffa crates was waiting for Dad outside the house.

'Make the most of these,' Granddad said. 'If it goes like the last war, anything from abroad will soon stop coming through.'

'But you get your fruit from Covent Garden,' I pointed out.

He laughed. 'Where do you think they get it from? Most of it comes over in ships and planes from where they have better weather than us.'

'Where's that?' I asked.

'Just about bloody everywhere at the moment!'

It took the rest of the day to get most of the windows covered. That was the downside of living in a big house. But, with a base-ment level, and three floors above, Dad's ladders would only get so high. For the top two floors he used black paint direct on the glass. At least during the day you could open them.

As darkness fell, I noticed that the lamps stayed unlit. The lamplighter normally came round our area around seven or eight. By ten o'clock there was no sign. And no sign of anything else either. Standing on our front step – door closed, of course, to keep the light in – it felt like we were back in the country again. All around was dark with just tall shapes looming out of the shad-ows. If I hadn't spent so many weeks in a pitch-black common I might have been scared. In fact, I was just interested. It was just another thing that happened.

By the time I was in bed, however, that changed. My head was filled with the idea of strangers trying to kill us. I didn't know what a bomb or a German looked like. By the time I ran sweating into my parents' room, they'd become picture-book ogres in my head. I was convinced we were going to die.

There were other changes. Some of these were more fun, on the face of it, anyway. In fact, the 'face' was the first place I saw a change. While we were away, Granddad had taken delivery of a large box addressed to us. Inside were lots of smaller cardboard boxes, one for each of us. Dad told us to be careful opening them, but I was nine years old.

The smell hit me first. After six weeks of nature, the whiff of rubber was like a punch on the nose. It was so artificial and nasty. In the country, everything smells as it should do. I even grew to like the stench of horse manure. Mum had been right. It really did smell 'fresh'. But whatever was in these boxes had not come from the earth.

If they smelled weird, there was no word for what they looked like.

'They're gas masks,' Dad said, although he seemed to have as much clue as the rest of us about what to do with them. A little beige card in the box gave instructions. What we had was a 'respirator' and a 'transparent eyepiece'. What they looked like was a rubber hat with a face like welders' goggles.

The instructions told us how to put them on. Mine was red,

like all the kids'. Mum and Dad had black ones. Even my new brother, Peter, had a version that fitted over his whole head and shoulders like a fish tank. They pulled a bit on the back of my hair, as short as it was, but the worst thing was the stink. Dad said they were to protect us from breathing in poisonous gases. It felt to me like they were pumping it out.

But that was all forgotten when I tried to speak. It was like trying to speak at the bottom of the canal. Listening to the others try was even funnier and in the end we were all laughing. If there's an upside to having to face a life-threatening situation then I think we found it.

Eventually Dad took his off and told us all to pack ours away. We were to keep them with us at all times, he instructed.

'Do not lose them – these funny-looking things could save your lives.'

Only if the Germans laughed themselves to death looking at us, I thought. But that night, left to my own thoughts again, I began to dwell on what was happening and it wasn't long before my thoughts turned dark again. It was all well and good having a laugh at the gas masks but it was time to admit why we'd been sent them in the first place. They weren't just a present from the War Office to make us smile. They were intended to save our lives.

I couldn't get my head around that.

I'm Alfie Dole, Pearly Prince of St Pancras. I'm only nine years old. Why would Mr Hitler want to kill me?

There were other changes too. I started to notice posters on the side of shops or at bus stops. Some reminded us to keep the lights down at night – 'black means black' – which was okay unless you were one of the lucky ones with a car or walking along the road. Driving in pitch-black was going to be no fun for anyone. There was another poster with a picture of a gas mask. 'Hitler will send no warning,' it informed us. 'Always carry your gas mask.'

I patted my coat pocket. There it was, as usual.

The gas mask wasn't the only thing waiting for me when I got home from Kent. During one of his weekdays back in London Dad had signed up the whole family to the rationing list. By the time we were back, we all had a little card-covered book with our names and addresses on. There was also a registration number as well. My book was blue. Wally, being under five, had a green one. The adults got a boring beige colour.

If the gas masks had to be looked after, these books were like gems to be hoarded away. In fact, I wasn't even allowed to keep mine.

'I'll be looking after these,' Mum said, whipping them out of our hands.

Over the next day or two we all went to various butchers and grocers to register our books. From now on, these would be the only places we could shop, and each time we'd have to produce our books or no sale. No wonder Mum wanted to keep them safe.

Rationing hit everyone hard but, I suppose, in a way the richer families suffered more than us. My little book was the maximum that I could buy and eat in one week. The truth was, when we looked at the amount of meat we were allowed to purchase, it wasn't far off what we would eat normally, whereas wealthy people would have been used to having the pick of whatever they wanted. I was more affected by things like eggs, which we ate a lot of. Restrictions on those affected me directly.

As a kid, though, I got preferential treatment over Mum and Dad. That's why my book was a different colour. Milk was something else on the list but all kids were entitled to half a pint a day. The government also wanted us to have the full meat, fruit and veg quotas.

As it turned out, fruit and veg weren't affected by rationing so I thought Granddad's shop would be okay. That wasn't the case. When I went in No. 151 a few weeks later, I couldn't help notice it was looking sparse. Then he told me 80 per cent of UK fruit was imported from overseas. The odds of much of it making the journey now were slim.

'Why?'

'U-boats.'

This war was getting worse. It was so hard to comprehend as a kid. It's not much easier now. First Adolf was going to poison me. Now he was shooting fruit on boats. It just didn't make sense. Even when Granddad kept reminding me that there were men and women on these ships at danger, I knew they weren't the target. Who aims torpedoes at fruit?

His stock might not have been rationed officially but getting hold of it quickly became a problem. Covent Garden, when I next went with him, was like a ghost ship. The porters were leaning on barrows and the wholesalers looked a bit pathetic. What they had, they had a lot of – like potatoes and leeks – but the fruit side of things was poor. When he did buy something, Granddad had to fill in various forms to prove it was going to the right place.

Still, while he had stock, Granddad did his best to make sure it went to the right people. It didn't matter how much money you had, families with young children got preferential treatment over adults. Like the others in his trade, he could have made more money by hiking the prices, but where was the fairness in that? He didn't own a supermarket and live miles away. He was part of the community. People relied on him. What's more, people have long memories. He didn't know how long the war would last but if he messed his customers around now they'd go elsewhere as soon as they could.

Having the government tell us what we could eat was one thing. But they weren't paying for it. When the war started we were worse off than ever. The hopping money went only so far but then we had to rely on Dad again. With the threat of bombers overhead any moment, the demand for painters and decorators was nonexistent. Building work dried up as well. All the work he'd done on St Francis House and the other yellow-bricks on Bridgeway and the white blocks on Ossulston had come to an end. Even labouring for a pittance was hard to come by.

Granddad wasn't the only person affected by Germans taking pot shots at fruit and veg. Mum's Sunday stall business ground to a halt in the cold months. What with Dad's income being up in the air, there was nothing else for it. She had to get a job.

Obviously there were ramifications for the family. Dad was in and out and Dave, by now, had escaped to his own job (he liked school as much as me). So if Grandma or an aunt couldn't help, that left me and Rosie to look after the young ones. I hated Mum for going to work.

But that was before I discovered *where* she was working.

The Tolmer was a yellow-brick cinema tucked inside Tolmer's Square, a cul-de-sac over the Euston Road from Warren Street. It had been built as a church but for whatever reason it was converted into a theatre, although when Mum joined as an usherette they still had the bell tower on the roof. Inside it was a real fleapit of a place, as far from God as you can get with your sticky seats and rowdy crowd. But people loved it. This was where those who could afford it could watch the Pathé News on a Saturday or a double-bill at nights. It's where, for example, they would have played the film of Henry Croft's funeral. They were all silent films, of course, so at the front was a giant Wurlitzer organ.

How do I know? Because as soon as Mum had her foot in the door she let the whole family in whenever we wanted. The kids' features on a Saturday were packed with Doles, but I'd watch anything. The technology behind it all was fascinating. I'd heard of televisions, although never seen one. This was the closest I'd get to moving pictures until TVs became widely available in the '50s.

I wasn't the only kid who got in for free. The 'tuppenny rush' – when they let children in for a reduced price – was the most popular time of the week. Every Saturday the square would be packed with kids. As soon as the usher opened the foyer doors, they'd rush in. Some of them stopped to buy tickets, but usually there were too many pushing through to count. Mum refused to work this shift, saying, 'It's not worth the bruises.'

It wasn't just the kids who could get a bit unruly. For some people the films seemed to be an afterthought, particularly if it was a late screening. That's when beer might have played a part and fights might kick off. There was something about the place that made people think they could tear up if they wanted. Maybe it was the cheap price. Maybe they were letting off steam because of being at war. All I knew is, even on the worst nights, when there was a mass brawl over some stupid thing and beer bottles got lobbed around, the organist never lost his place in the film. The show had to go on!

Mum liked being at the Tolmer less than I did. Sometimes people would leave behind purses or wallets, though, and, depending on how they'd behaved, she'd either hand it in or take it home. That was her own little justice system. Again, tidying up after kids had been in got on her nerves. If she could bring anything home to share with us, then she would.

She would have chucked it in if she could, but Dad's situation had changed again. His – and our – worst fears had come true. The letter had arrived telling him that he had been conscripted. We were going to lose our dad.

Even though fighting hadn't actually happened outside of Poland, you got the feeling it was just a matter of time. Because of his building background, Dad was called up for the Pioneer Corps, a new unit that was basically the engineering arm of the military. But it wasn't all constructing and labouring. The Pioneers were used as front-line forces to clear obstructions for the land troops. They would be the first battalion the enemy saw. The Pioneers' badge was a pick, shovel and gun. They used to say, the gun to shoot yourself and the pick and shovel to dig your own grave – not necessarily in that order.

As a consequence, it wasn't enough that he knew his way around electrics and plumbing. He needed infantry training and that could only take place away from London. We all cried when he left, even Mum, who could normally put a brave face on anything that didn't involve a mouse. Even though he was only going down to Aldershot, it was for six weeks. A lot could happen in six weeks. When we'd left London in August it was peacetime. When we came back we were at war. Who knew, really, what was going to happen?

Those six weeks were hard but, at the end of them, Dad did return. Apparently he'd been in the same unit as England cricketer Denis Compton, which had been entertaining if confusing, as he was only twenty-odd and the Pioneers was usually where they put the old boys.

Compton would take the mickey out of Dad when they were doing exercises.

'Come on, Alf, get your feet up.'

'It's all right for you, Compton, you're a young man. I could get my feet up when I was your age.'

Compton aside, I don't think there were many other laughs because everyone knew what they were training for. In any case, Dad wasn't about to discuss it with us kids.

The 'Phoney War', they called it. The newspapers, people in pubs, the porters down at Covent Garden, they were all talking about how we were all getting ready for something that wasn't happening. But, Dad pointed out, you try telling that to the families of the people being killed at sea by the U-boats.

'There's nothing phoney about their war,' he said.

Even so, the worst thing that happened to us was the not knowing. We had gas masks in case there was poison, we had ration books in case the food ran out, we blacked out our windows in case the light in the front room led the Nazis to our doors. But in the time we'd been back from Kent, all that had really happened in Somers Town is that everyone just worried a lot more.

Something was going to happen, though. Everyone was sure of that. The fact the government was already rolling out the delivery of free Anderson Shelters merely confirmed it. As Dad said, 'For Chamberlain and his mob to give us anything tells you how serious it is.'

Not everyone got the freebie. As I recall, ours was only buckshee because Dad wasn't earning £5 a week at the time. Anyone on more than that had to pay £7. If you didn't have a yard to put it in, then they erected public ones out on the street. It all sounded very clever to me and then the men arrived with ours and I was left scratching my head.

Six sheets of 78-inch by 54-inch corrugated iron were paraded through our house on Werrington Street to the back yard. I kept waiting for something, for the thing that was going to make them proper safe. But it never came. I couldn't work it out. Basically all we'd been given was the world's first flat-pack furniture. How was this pile of flimsy metal meant to be safer than our massive house made of bricks?

The men had a look round the yard and indicated a patch by the back wall where we had a few veggies growing.

'That's your best spot.'

'On my spuds?' Dad asked.

'Safest place is against the wall, with the mud over the top.'

'If you say so.'

So that was another casualty of this phoney war – our Sunday roast.

All the men on the street who were still around chipped in to help each other. First of all, they dug out an area by the wall, going down nearly four feet, then they bolted the sheets of metal together until they'd got an archway built over the area. There were panels at the front and back, one end with a door. Then they shovelled all the spare earth and more over the top of the shelter and piled it high as a barrier at the door for extra protection and insulation. That made it hard for Dad to get inside but scurrying up the mound of mud to get in made it all the more fun for me and Wal.

It looked good, exciting even. But I was still none the wiser how this would be safer than being indoors.

When the men had finished in our garden, Dad left with them to do next door's. Meanwhile I helped Mum with the inside. It was dark and already musty and bound to be cold, so the first thing we did was cut some lino to fit the floor and put some wood and paper around the sides. Then we put in boxes of blankets and sheets, some crates to sit on and eat from, and even some tinned food. Basically, all the little things you need if you're going to stay out of the house for any period of time.

'Just in case,' Mum said.

Rosie and I couldn't wait for the hard work to be finished. All we wanted to do was play in there. Of course, it was different games. She wanted to set up a little home for her and her friends and their dolls. I wanted to pretend I was hunting in the jungle or chasing bad guys through the forest. The shelter was my hideout.

Some of our neighbours found it hard to get their shelters ship-shape. They were the ones who'd never been hopping. We helped Mum do this to a hut not much bigger every year. It was just like going on holiday again for us.

But still nothing happened. Conditions got worse, Granddad's shop was full one minute, bereft of anything but empty boxes the next, and school was even harder because all anyone could talk about was the war. Actually, though, there wasn't much to stop us living our normal lives. Granddad even started doing his Pearly collections again and encouraged me to go with him as much as possible. If anything, he said, people needed us more than ever.

As spring turned to summer 1940, any opportunities to perform were taken out of my hands. The first I knew was when I saw Mum in my room with a little case. Beside it was a pile of my things including my gas mask, toothbrush, flannel and pyjamas. Next to that was a sheet of paper containing a list she seemed to be ticking off. A suitcase usually only meant one thing.

'Is it hopping time already, Mum?' I asked.

She looked up at me and shook her head.

'I'm sorry, darling, I wish we were going there.'

'So why are we packing?'

'I don't know how to tell you this, Boy-Boy, but they're taking you away.'

13

He's Not One of Ours

Saturday 15 June 1940. It wasn't a school day but the playground was full. Everyone from my class and the years above and below me was there and pretty much all of them were or had been crying. I know I had. I didn't want to be sent away but Mum said it was for my own good. The Nazis had overrun France, the only country between us and Germany. It was only a matter of time, the newspapers were saying, before they made their way over the Channel to us. And where would they head? London.

'So that's why you can't be here,' Mum said, tear stains on her face as well. She looked around at us. 'None of you can.'

Apart from David, who was too old, and Peter, who was too young, we were all there. Me, Wally, Marjorie and Rosie. All carrying our little cases, all dressed in our caps and coats, even though it was summer, and all with address labels attached to our collars like we were parcels going in the post. I looked at mine.

'London County Council', it said at the top, then there was a space for my name and school. On the back there was the address of where I was being sent. All it had was one word: 'Wales'.

I looked at the others. Wally's sign said 'Norfolk', Marj's 'Wiltshire' and Rosie's, I was pleased to see, said 'Wales' too.

'We'll be able to see each other,' she said.

'I wouldn't get your hopes up,' Mum said. 'It's a big place. A whole country, in fact.'

Officially we were the second wave of evacuees. The first exodus of children and the ill or elderly had taken place even before war was declared the previous August. But with the war so phoney for so long, most children had returned. Despite the government having so many posters up advertising it, Mum and Dad had decided not to split the family up back then. They were right to. Nothing happened except families were ripped apart for nothing.

Now, things were different. Hitler was progressing, his troops were moving. The last place Mum and Dad wanted us was in the line of fire. They didn't know where we were going and they had no say in it, not even to try to keep us together. But even alone and miserable had to be better than under attack at home in the capital city.

After about an hour of queuing and having our names checked and double-checked by men and women with clipboards, we were all told to get into pairs then we were led out of the playground and into Chalton Street. As soon as we turned right at the bottom I knew where we were heading: Euston Station. Wherever Wales was, that was how I got there.

If it had been hard at the playground, saying goodbye to Mum at the station was harrowing. We were all crying and so was she.

'When are we going to see you again?' I called out through a crack at the top of the train window.

'When it's safe,' she replied.

'Well, when will that be?'

'I don't know, love, I don't know.'

As the train started to move, Mum called out, 'You're the oldest, Alfie. Look after them.'

Then her voice was lost among the wheeze and chuff of steam-powered pistons and we were on our own.

I might be the oldest, I thought, *but I'm only ten years old – and I want my mummy.*

We were in the system now. I didn't know anything about the rail network, so I assumed we were on the right train. When it stopped shortly after leaving the station I knew I was wrong. More officials with registers came through the carriages checking our tags. One look at Walter's and he was told to get his case and follow them.

'I don't want to!' he screamed. 'Rosie, don't let them take me.'

He flung himself at his older sister but there was nothing she could do. Nothing any of us could do. Strong adult arms scooped him and his luggage up and lifted him out of the car. And then there were three.

An hour or more later the rest of the Doles were turfed out as well. The sign at the station said Birmingham. We were told to wait by another platform for further instruction. By now we were starving. The government letter had said to pack some barley sugar but Mum hadn't. We hadn't had a crumb since breakfast.

The noise on the platform was terrifying. It was like having ten schools all shouting at each other at once. Even I was cowed by the volume and I liked a shout as much as anyone. Only when a whistle blew did kids begin to quieten. We were told to get into groups when our names were read out. This took almost another hour. There were so many children on the platform that I thought we'd definitely lose a few onto the tracks. The fact we didn't was more luck than judgement. I made sure me, Marj and Rosie were in the middle just in case.

After what seemed like an age, the crowd began to thin as children started appearing on different platforms. As trains began pulling in, being loaded with crying kids, then pulling out, I wondered how anyone else was getting around. I didn't know anything about evacuation but I did know that unless you were under fourteen and leaving home for a while, you wouldn't be getting a train anywhere for a while because we had them all.

Eventually I heard the word 'Dole' and managed to prick up my ears long enough to hear which platform to head to. By now Marjie was asleep on the ground. We shook her awake and told her the good news: she was coming with us. How far, I couldn't say. Wiltshire and Wales might be next door to each other for all I knew, or they might be a thousand miles apart.

Before we boarded we were given the chance to use the toilet. This used up another half-hour. But the train seemed to be in no hurry. When the big engines roared into life, however, it was a different story. As steam billowed into the air, threatening to swallow the driver's cab and beyond, the porters became animated, blowing whistles and shepherding tiny bodies along the platform and into open doors.

I was out of breath by the time we got on board. Luckily my sisters and I found seats together, in the corner of a bench seat. I put our cases underneath. As we pulled out of the station there was silence in the carriage as ten or so kids stared out longingly. No one knew where Birmingham was, no one called it home. But we all felt that leaving there was symbolic. It signified to all of us that we were heading further away from our families.

I knew about the logic behind the evacuation. I'd seen the posters at Euston Station. One had a picture of a brother and sister — it could have been me and Rosie — with the words: 'Mothers: send them out of London. Give them a chance of greater safety and health.' Another one had a cartoon of a boy helping clear some wreckage and a man saying, 'Leave this to us, sonny — you ought to be out of London.' As we trundled along the track, surrounded by trees and countryside either side, I realised that common sense counted for nothing. Why had Mum and Dad sent us this time and not the last year when so many other kids went? Was it more dangerous now or did they just want us out of their hair for a while?

By the time we'd been moving for half an hour I'd convinced myself we'd been abandoned.

Only the sight of Marjorie looking unhappier than me stopped me breaking down completely. Other kids weren't so thoughtful. A round-faced boy in a smart blazer spotted my sister's tears and started laughing.

'What a baby!' he said, pointing his finger and encouraging everyone else to join in. 'Too afraid to be without Mummy, are you?'

'Leave it out,' I said. 'She's only young.'

'Leave it out,' the boy mimicked me. 'She's only young!' For some reason he found that hilarious. The other kids in the carriage weren't so sure but one boy, clearly the ringleader's brother judging by his moon-shaped face, guffawed loudly enough for all of them. That was it.

'The next one who laughs at my sister gets it,' I said.

'Don't,' Rosie said.

'Or what?' the first boy asked. 'Are you going to cry as well?'

Right . . .

I wasn't Alf Dole's boy for nothing. The kid was still laughing when I clocked him one on the nose. A second later, as blood burst out all over his smart blazer, he wasn't seeing the funny side any more. I stayed upright and stared at his brother.

'Anyone else laughing?' I asked.

If the boy stood up he'd be bigger and certainly heavier than me. I was banking on him being a coward. Most loudmouths, Dad used to tell me, were all talk.

'No, you're all right,' the brother said. 'It was just a joke.'

'Well, it's not a funny one,' I spat back.

The next few minutes passed in torturous silence. I wasn't sure if Rosie was cross with me or not but Marjorie was staring at me with new-found admiration. I winked at her and then she smiled. That was worth more to me than winning a fight.

By the time we were aware of the train slowing down, the atmosphere in the carriage was back to normal with the other kids gossiping and laughing again – but not at upset little girls. Only Nosebleed continued to glare at me when he thought I wasn't looking. When we pulled into a station everyone listened out for the announcement. My heart sank when I realised Rosie and I were getting off – but Marjorie was staying on. After our good-byes I turned to the boys left in the carriage.

'Anyone upsets my sister and I'll hear about it, all right?'

But if I was expecting trouble from the brothers, that was unlikely. Nosebleed got off with us. Behind him his brother was blubbing for all he was worth. When I got onto the platform Nosebleed was sobbing as well. I could have made a fuss but what was the point? The truth was, no one was happy. We might have been sent away for our health and safety but no one seemed to care about our emotions. I would have given anything to have been back in London with my family. And so, I bet, would every single kid on that train and platform.

There was another wait then another train and then we did the whole thing over again, except this time it was just me. Rosie got off and for an hour I carried on to a place called Merthyr Tydfil. That, according to the man with the clipboard, was the end of the line for me.

'Go and stand over there, Dole,' one of the clipboards instructed. 'Your new parents will be along presently.'

'I've already got parents,' I said defiantly. But, I wondered, would I ever see them again?

They sound funny.

That was my first impression of Mr and Mrs Davies. Yes, I

noticed that she was small and mousey with brown hair in a bun under her yellow bonnet, and he was short and broad, but not fat like the kids on the train. He looked solid, like a bull. But it was their voices that fascinated me as we walked the mile to their house. Everything they said sounded like they were about to break into a song.

Granddad's accent is different but this one's just silly.

Only when a few people had stopped to chat and ask whether I was the boy from London did I realise that everyone was like it. It sounded friendly, I suppose. But I noticed that the adults only spoke about me and pointed in my direction. None of them addressed me directly. It was like the Davieses were coming back from market with a new pig.

I wondered how Wally and the others were getting on. *I hope it's nicer than this.*

That changed when we got to their house. I'd seen countryside before, so the open fields and the trees and the hills in the distance didn't impress me as much as I think the Davieses were hoping. But when I saw their house my mouth dropped open. It was standing on its own at the end of a little path. There were no flats above it and no other buildings joined to its sides. It was small but it had everything right there. Maybe I was going to be all right.

Inside wasn't too dissimilar to home. There was a scullery and front room. The tin bath hung inside the kitchen, just like I was used to. Upstairs was different. In fact the stairs themselves were odd as well. I was used to a long line, fifteen or so, straight up. These wound themselves around a post in the ground. The ceiling had beams across it like in Kitty's stable. They were low, as well. Mr Davies wasn't tall but he only just cleared the criss-crossed wood.

I was shown to my room. It was plain, with a bed, a bowl for washing, a wardrobe and a dresser. I only had eyes, however, for the window. I could see straight out, over the trees in the garden, to a river and, behind that, hills that were so tall they looked like mountains. I couldn't wait to get out there and explore.

Mr D went back downstairs while his wife said she'd help me unpack. Still staring out the window, I heard the click of my case clasp and turned to see her lifting my possessions out onto the bed.

'Oh my word,' she exclaimed. 'Mr Davies, will you come and look at this!'

There was the crunch of his heavy feet on the winding stairs and then Mr D appeared in the doorway. His wife was holding my gas mask.

'Have you ever seen anything so frightening?' she asked him. 'Well, Alfred, you won't be needing it here, I can promise you that.'

She put it on the dresser, next to my torch and toothbrush, then she started on my clothes. Mr Davies was barely halfway back down the stairs when she hollered for him to come back up.

'What now?' he asked.

'Look at this!' This time she was laughing. 'My goodness, his parents must hate him more than I thought if they make the boy wear this!' When I turned to look I felt the anger rise. She was holding up my Pearly suit – my new one, because the original was too small. Dad had told me to bring it to treat my hosts. But they were just poking fun at it and therefore at me, at Dad, at Granddad and at Henry Croft.

I knew at that moment I would never wear it in front of them, even if they begged. And what was that crack about Mum and Dad 'hating' me? I decided to pick Mrs D up on it over supper.

'Well,' she said, 'they've sent you away for a reason, haven't they?'

'It's to keep us safe,' I said. I was sure about that.

'You think what you like, dear. I know the truth. Now eat your meal.'

To her credit, Mrs Davies was a great cook. We had pheasant and roast vegetables, things only rich people had at home. But I couldn't enjoy it as much as it deserved. My host's words had left a bitter taste in my mouth and I was glad when I was finally sent up to bed after washing up.

'Hope you're not afraid of the dark,' Mr Davies laughed. 'It's a bit different out here in the country.'

'We have night-time in London,' I said.

'Maybe, but not like this.'

He was right, but not in the way he hoped. Outside the window it couldn't have been blacker if I'd closed my eyes. But after nearly a year of blackouts on Werrington Street, I was used to that. If Mr D thought I was going to be scared of the darkness, he was going to be disappointed.

But what was different was the sky. It was full of stars, twinkling and flickering, glowing and sparkling. Of course I'd seen stars before, especially down in Kent, but never like this. Never so clear and so many.

I went to sleep, dreaming I could fly.

Monday at home would have been a school day. The last thing I expected in Wales was for it to be the same. But it was. Mrs Davies went through my clothes and dug out the best outfit she could for school. I could tell she wasn't impressed. Finally she settled on a pair of shorts and a shirt with my grey cap.

'That'll have to do,' she sighed, 'but you'll have to clean your boots.'

An hour later, after a breakfast of eggs and toast, she walked me back towards the station. On the way we saw other kids, most walking without adults. The school had to be close.

Mr Cooper was the teacher. He showed me to a desk and introduced me to a few other boys. Then he told everyone to start writing with their pencils while he went to talk to Mrs Davies. When he returned, I was holding another kid against the wall.

'Dole!' he yelled. 'This is not how we do things in Wales!'

'But he hit me, sir,' I said, not taking my eyes off the kid.

'I don't want to hear it,' he said, snatching my arm away from the boy's collar. 'Now, you are a guest here so I'm going to let you off this time. But step out of line once more and you will know about it. Do you understand?'

I nodded.

'I said, do you understand?'

'Yes.'

'Yes, what?'

'Yes, Mr Cooper.'

'Fine. Now return to your seat. I hope you're going to impress us all with your knowledge of history after that performance.'

I knew I couldn't impress anyone. I also knew I wouldn't fit into that school. I was a stranger and they all wanted to make sure I knew it.

After school it only got worse. I had to find my own way home, which was fine because I got to walk off the road and kick around through the bushes. When I got in, Mrs D had a list of chores for me, including mowing the lawn and pruning her rose bushes. Again, that was fine. Anything outdoors suited me. It all started to go wrong when the man of the house came home. I was still out the back with the gardening scissors when he came round the side. I must have jumped because he laughed.

'Never seen a bit of soot before, boyo?' he called out. I had, but not like this. He was covered face to toe. A consequence, he said, of working down the mines.

He went inside then about twenty minutes later I was called in as well. I expected it was to have tea. What I didn't expect was to find the giant bulk of Mr D squeezed into the tin bath in front of the fire and him holding out a hard pumice stone for me.

'Scrub my back, would you, and make sure you get it all out.'

It was disgusting. I didn't mind the coal dust, which had some-how found its way inside his clothes. But his skin was revolting to touch and, in any case, I didn't even know him. Mrs D carried on cooking like we weren't there.

Every day after work I had to do that. For the first time in my life I found myself wanting to stay at school, just so I'd get home and find Mr D already clean. What had he done before I'd arrived? Mrs D must have scrubbed him. Why couldn't she do it now?

Then I'd go to school the next day and hate that as well. I knew that term ended in July in London. I wondered if Wales had the same rules. I hoped they did.

After two weeks of the same routine something changed. I was walking to school when I saw a familiar shape ahead of me.

It can't be . . .?

A second later it had vanished but I knew what I had seen. I started running down the hill, as fast as I could in my outsized boots, pushing through the dawdling throng until I got to the school gate. And there she was: my sister Rosie.

I ran up and gave her a hug. She burst into tears. The woman holding her hand looked as confused as anything.

'Do you two know each other?'

'He's my big brother, Mrs Jones!' Rosie squealed. 'Can he come and stay with us as well?'

Mrs Jones looked like she'd rather have Hitler as a houseguest than some ragamuffin with coal under his nails. But she smiled and said, 'It's not up to me, Rosemary. I'm sure your brother has his own nice family.'

'I haven't,' I blurted. 'They're horrible to me.'

Mrs Jones tutted and dragged Rosie away. 'I need to get you registered,' she said.

I saw my sister again at lunchtime. She told me the Joneses were nice and they'd wanted her to settle in before going to school. That's why she'd had a fortnight's break.

'My lot wanted me out of their hair the second I arrived. They hate me.'

'Just do one of your Pearly turns. They'll love that.'

I blushed. 'I don't think so. They saw my suit and just laughed.'

'Oh.'

After school I tried to see her again but Mrs Jones collected her early. No one would tell me where they lived so I couldn't follow. The next day was the same. We got five minutes together before school, half an hour at lunch, a minute or two at break and then Rosie was whisked away. I couldn't understand why we weren't allowed to see each other when we were living so close. Why couldn't we live together? I decided to ask Mrs Davies. As usual, she laughed in my face.

'They're not paying me enough for you, let alone two of you!'

'Who's paying you?' I asked. It was the first I'd heard.

'The government, who else? Do you think we'd have you lot in our houses for nothing?'

I hadn't thought of that.

'Well, if I'm so expensive then I'll move out,' I snapped.

More laughter.

'Chance would be a fine thing. Now, start getting that bath ready for Mr Davies.'

But I'd decided. That night I packed my case and threw it out of the window into the bush below. The following morning I picked it up on the way to school and stuffed in my toothbrush and pyjamas. So long, Davieses. I wouldn't be coming back.

At school I hid my case just outside the wall then went and found Rosie.

'Meet me at the gate at break.'

'Why?'

'We're running away.'

'Where?'

'Home.'

'But we don't know how to get there.'

'Then we'll have to find out.'

It all went according to plan. We made it as far as the station before Rosie even mentioned her case.

'Maybe I could just go back? Mrs Jones won't be in.'

That took another half an hour. Eventually we made it onto the platform. When a guard walked over we pretended to be asleep. According to the sign, we had another fifteen minutes for a train to Liverpool. I didn't know where that was but it had to be closer to London than here.

Twelve minutes later I was managing to peer out from under my cap. I could hear the train pulling into the station. If we timed it right we could be on and hiding before the guard noticed we were missing. I watched the train stop and the doors fling outwards as people spilled off.

'Come on, Rosie,' I said. 'It's time.'

We grabbed our luggage and ran over to one of the open doors. I threw my case in and was just about to hop up when I felt a hand on my shoulder. The guard had seen us.

Except it wasn't the guard. It was Mrs Davies.

'Going somewhere?' she asked, smiling but without looking at all happy.

'We're going home,' I said.

'How right you are,' she agreed, and dragged me back from the train. 'Except your home is up the hill with me and Mr Davies.'

Behind her I saw Mrs Jones running across. She looked more humiliated than angry. Rosie would probably just get another hug from her. I, on the other hand, would probably have to wash Mr Davies twice as punishment, and again on Sunday when he wasn't even working.

We ran away twice more. Each time we were caught before we managed to step onto the train or bus. Each time Mrs Davies smacked me on the legs as soon as we were out of sight of anyone else and each time she reminded me, 'You're only here because no one else wants you!'

I knew that wasn't true but I had no way to prove it except by asking my parents. And if no one was letting me go home, how could I do that?

Then, after about six or seven weeks, after a busy summer holiday morning of climbing trees and fishing in the River Taff, I came home for lunch to be met by Mrs D standing with her arms folded. She didn't look pleased.

'The Nazis are bombing Cardiff,' she announced. 'Your parents have asked for you to go home.'

'See, I told you they wanted me!'

She didn't answer, just threw my case and coat out of the door at me.

'I know you can find the station on your own.'

Then she slammed the door and that was the last I ever saw of her.

*

I was so happy to be leaving I didn't dare dream of Rosie, but when I reached the station there she was on the platform with Mr and Mrs Jones. They seemed like genuinely nice people and she hugged them both warmly before she said goodbye. Then a man with a clipboard appeared out of nowhere and, along with some other kids who'd arrived from God knows where, he put us all in the same carriage. Then he went round us all handing out tags for us to loop around our buttonholes again. When it was my turn to use the pencil to fill in my name I noticed that the tag already had one word printed on it in large capital letters: 'LONDON'.

I smiled. It was true. I was really going home.

It was a brief family reunion when we finally got there and not the one I expected. Grandma Emma and two of my aunts met us at the station. Mum had already done the run earlier in the day to pick up Wally after his stay in Norfolk but now she needed to work. When I got home I spent ages just wandering around the house, smelling it, touching it, remembering all the good times I'd had in it. I knew it wouldn't be long before we moved again but wherever my family was, that was home. I never wanted to be split up from them again.

When my parents came home, I don't know who was more glad. Tears went round the room like wildfire. We were all so glad to be back. That's when I noticed someone was missing.

'When's Marjie coming home?' I asked.

Mum looked at Dad and he just stared at the floor.

'Mum?'

She coughed and stood up.

'The thing is,' Dad began, 'Marjorie went to a lovely place in Wiltshire where Hitler is never going to find her. And she is having such a lovely time with a man and woman who can't have children of their own that we decided to leave her there for a while.'

I heard his words but they weren't making sense to me. So what about Hitler? We needed to be together. A child's place was with her family. Her *real* family – not this pair of strangers.

'Doesn't Marjorie want to come home?' I asked.

Dad sighed.

'No,' he said. 'I'm afraid she doesn't.'

Whatever he said after that was drowned out by the sound of my sobbing. What had we done wrong? Was it because of the bullying on the train? I'd done my best to protect her, I really had. Had she decided to stay away because of me?

Dad kneeled next to me and wrapped his arms around me.

'It's no one's fault,' he said. 'She'll be home soon enough.'

I didn't know it then but I had seen my little sister for the very last time.

Before the news about Marjorie had really sunk in, there was another blow to family life. Even as Mum and Dad decided to bring us back from our evacuation, other kids were being sent away as the Nazis sounded the death knell on the phoney war. German planes had attacked British warships in the Channel and the first dogfight in UK airspace had taken place. It was the first stage of the invasion that we'd all been dreading. Operation Sea Lion, Hitler called it. Operation Get Your Family Together Then Get Them Out Of London was Dad's interpretation.

'They're attacking the airfields and the ports,' Dad said one night at dinner, 'but it's only a matter of time before they come for the capital, so you can't stay here.'

He looked round at us. 'I'm going away in two days with the Pioneers. Tomorrow I'm driving you all down to Kent in Granddad's lorry. You'll be safe there.'

How was he to know?

As we got out of the van and started unloading the furniture, there was a fizzing noise above us. Three small grey aeroplanes with yellow nose and wing tips were flying over the site, one of them low enough for us to see the pilot's face.

I couldn't help punching the air and waving.

Dad grabbed my arm.

'Don't do that, Boy-Boy,' he said grimly. 'He's not one of ours.'

14

They're Here

Mum was hysterical.

'No, no, no!' she cried. 'Not here as well.'

Bore Green Farm was supposed to be our sanctuary. London was the target, that's why we'd escaped. What did Adolf want with a few hops and spuds?

The good news was that Paddock Wood wasn't a target. Not as far as Dad could work out from talking to the farmer and the families who'd been there a while. The bad news was that it was close enough to the ports and London for bombers en route to occasionally fly overhead.

'I'm an idiot,' Dad scolded himself. 'I should have thought of this.'

'Trust me, you're still safer here than in the city,' the farmer said. 'I listen to the BBC. It's only a matter of time.'

Dad decided to take him at his word. There wasn't much else he could do. After a day with us, he had to get back to the

Pioneers. Mum tried to hold it together as he left but with the Luftwaffe buzzing overhead it was impossible to cover up what everyone was thinking.

This might be the last time we see him.

Because we were there early the hops weren't ready to pick. The stiltsmen hadn't started clipping the bind yet. Once we'd collected firewood in the morning there weren't any other chores so Mum let us off to play. It was going to be weird without Marjorie but we'd do our best. As the others hared off, Mum called me back.

'It would help us out if we had a nice trout tonight,' she said.

'I'll see what I can do.'

Some of the other families caught on and soon there were rows of fishermen up and down the river and round the lake. I caught my fair share too. so we never went without. By Friday, however, as the trickle of menfolk – the ones who hadn't been drafted for whatever reason – started to arrive after their week's work, I found myself staring enviously at the meat they'd brought. That, in turn, made me think again of Dad being somewhere out there fighting for our country. I had to lose myself in the woods for ten minutes while the tears flowed. No one would have judged me but at ten years old I thought I should be able to put on a brave face for the young 'uns.

After the weekend, the Sunday male exodus started as usual. Goodbyes were hard for everyone. It was obvious a lot of fellas were leaving for combat or military service somewhere. Rather than shed any more tears I decided to go swimming where my wet eyes wouldn't be noticed. In any case, there was no bad time to go swimming. Or so I thought. For once, however, it was the wrong decision.

When I got back to the hut the kids were skipping around. Mum was at the fire with some of the other women cooking. The closer I got, the more I recognised the smoky aroma of chicken. I wondered who was the lucky family tonight. Only when I saw Mum turn the spit holding the bird did I begin to twig.

How is that ours? I wondered. *Where did it come from?*

Then I saw the answer coming out of our hut. It was Dad. He was wearing his usual brown trousers and a white vest with braces hanging down his back, like he was going for a shave. The Pioneer uniform was nowhere in sight.

'Dad!' I yelled, and bombed over as quickly as I could in my bare feet.

'Hello, Boy-Boy, I wondered when you'd show up.'

'What are you doing here?'

It was a flying visit, he said, but he had two bits of good news. The first was that he'd cashed in all our coupons in Chalton Street, so we had our week's rations of meat, eggs and milk. Even better, he'd been drafted out of the Pioneers and into the Fire Brigade. He was joining the watch down at Euston Road. With the planes already bombing the docks, they needed as many hands on the pumps as possible.

'Is it dangerous?' I worried.

'It's safer carrying a bucket than a gun.'

The upshot was, he could continue to live at home and,

whenever he got the opportunity, he could come down to visit, as long as the trains were working.

The hopping season officially started and we got to work. It was monotonous and hard as usual but at least it took our minds off what was going on in the skies. At least once a day we saw a squadron of planes fly over. It took a few seconds for anyone to work out whose side they were on. For those seconds, nobody breathed. In truth, though, it didn't matter whether they were Messerschmitts or Spitfires. We weren't the targets. The worst that could happen was if both sides were overhead at once. That meant there would be fighting and, most likely, casualties. Anyone down below could be in danger.

The first time I saw Spitfires in pursuit of the enemy, they were chasing a pack of Luftwaffe planes. Gunfire rattled from them all the way. We couldn't help cheering and whooping, especially when we saw smoke coming from the back of two of the German planes. I didn't think about what happened to those planes that had been hit. I didn't spare a second's thought for the pilots' lives. All I knew was that they were bad guys and they'd been sent packing by the RAF.

'I like wars,' I said.

That opinion didn't last long. The next time I saw Spitfires they were swooping and diving around Messerschmitts a few miles away. It was a clear day and a blue sky so we could see everything. My heart stopped when I saw one of them explode. I hadn't seen the colours so I didn't know whose side it was on. What if it was one of ours? I tried counting the ones left but they moved too fast. It didn't seem real. Men had just died before my eyes but they were so far away I couldn't take it in. In any case, I couldn't get upset until I knew whether or not they were German.

By the time we moved on to potato picking, news was reaching us that London had been under fire every night. At least we were safe for a few more weeks, but would our house still be there when we returned?

As it was, the house wasn't what I should have been worrying about. The imminent danger was closer to our temporary home.

We were crawling along the potato field as usual one day when I heard the unmistakeable drone of a single plane. When your back was aching from crouching all morning you were desperate for an excuse to stand up, have a stretch and look around the skies for one of our boys. It was a sunny day so I had to shield my eyes as I looked for where the noise was coming from. Then I saw it, a grey dot in the distance. A grey dot with distinctive flashes of yellow at its tip.

Why was a single German plane flying on its own? What were the Nazis up to now? Then I noticed the other colours, the oranges and reds and the dark, dark, black pouring from the back. The Messerschmitt was on fire.

And it was heading right for us.

All around me the women and children started screaming as the fiery grey missile grew larger in our vision as it came lower and closer. The noise sounded dreadful, like a million bees trying to get out of a jar. The farmer was on his tractor. Even he looked worried.

'It's gonna hit us!' he cried, and leaped out of his cab and onto the mud, face down.

Everyone else did the same. There was no time to run and nowhere safe to shelter. The plane was moving too fast to do anything but duck. I pulled Peter down into the mud with me and held on fast.

'We're gonna die, we're gonna die . . .'

Everyone was saying it. Then suddenly there was a huge dark shadow over our heads, the smell of smoke packed our lungs and our ears were filled with sound of the bees. I could feel the heat of the plane as it tore overhead.

But it didn't hit us. The second it had passed I was on my feet, just in time to see the plane somehow clear the wall to the edge of our farm and skip and bounce onto a field on the neighbouring land. Say what you like about the Germans, but that pilot knew how to land a plane in an emergency.

After that it was a sprint. All the kids raced towards the wall, desperate to get a glimpse of a real-life Nazi. Behind us the mums were screaming. I'm sure I could make out mine above the rest.

'Alfie! Rosie! Walter! Get back here! Get back here! It's not safe!'

We heard but we didn't listen. It was a race to get to the farm perimeter first. When I did, I instinctively jumped over it. Then I stopped. There was the plane, about two hundred yards from me, smoke still streaming from its engine where it must have been shot by a Spitfire over London. I could see the brown dents and tracks in the earth where it had bounced and braked to a halt. It had been a pretty amazing landing. Then the realisation hit me.

Somehow the pilot had managed to keep control. Which meant he was alive.

And still very, very dangerous.

That's why I stopped. Alongside me the other kids and some of the fitter mums had reached us as well. We all just huddled together, staring. No one knew what to do or where to go. Were we any safer here than ten yards further forward? What was a safe distance when you were near a flaming aircraft? Inside it was a man from the most evil country on earth. What hideous weapons would he be carrying?

Would he even look human?

I didn't know what Germans looked like. I'd never seen one. But the newspapers said they were monsters. Dad said it, too, so that's what he had to look like.

One thing was for sure.

He wouldn't have a pitchfork.

I couldn't believe it when a tractor came tearing through the field and stopped within feet of the wounded plane. The farmer leaped off, angry, shouting – and wielding a pitchfork like he was taking on a wild boar, not a soldier from the most terrifying armed forces on the planet. Yes, the fork had two deadly spikes that would corral any animal. But it was no match for a machine gun. Or a grenade or a sidearm or whatever other poisonous technology was stored in that cockpit.

The tension in the field was tangible. I swear I didn't breathe for three minutes. I couldn't. I'd never been so tense. Watching the farmer get out of the tractor and walk slowly over to the plane, jabbing with his weapon.

Then suddenly there was movement. The glass canopy on the plane slid back and two hands appeared in the air.

We cheered. The pilot was giving the same sign we all did when we played soldiers. He was surrendering.

Slowly he eased himself to his feet and clambered over the side and onto the floor, where he collapsed. The crash had taken it out of him. Behind me the cheers had subsided. We were confused, me as much as anyone. As the pilot took off his goggles and helmet I couldn't get over how much he looked like any of the men in Somers Town. He was just, so . . . so . . . normal. And yet here he was risking his own life to try to end ours.

When I raised it with Mum she said, 'You're too young to understand.' But I'm not sure she was any the wiser.

There was a party atmosphere that night. Both farms got together for a song and a dance and we relived the moment the world's most powerful military machine had been overpowered by a country bumpkin with two prongs on a stick. You could have heard the cheers in London. In fact, I couldn't wait to tell Dad all about it.

Psychologically, it gave everyone a lift. The Nazis, we realised, weren't unbeatable. And they weren't all monsters. They were just men and they could die like men, too.

So much for the safety of the countryside. But things were about to get worse. The Battle of Britain had been a strategic attack on the country's air capability. For some reason, the Nazis scaled back just when they were within an inch of winning. I suppose they never realised that. Instead they decided on a new approach, the indiscriminate terror bombing of London – it was time for the Blitz. After a year on the periphery, my war was about to get real.

It was the second time we'd returned to London from Kent since the war had started. This time felt more eerie than the first. Every road we came along showed some damage caused by a dropped bomb. Some houses had their roofs missing. Elsewhere there were gaps in a block of terraces where a house had just disappeared under a blast. From the outside it looked unnatural, like a smile with a missing tooth. At floor level there was a pile of wood and bricks and the odd bit of furniture. I didn't know how long it had been down but I had to look away. People would have been living in there. I hoped they'd reached their shelter in time.

When we swung into Werrington Street I was relieved to see our house was still standing. As soon as Mum unlocked the door I ran through to the yard. The Anderson shelter was still there as well, half-buried by mud. I crawled inside. It felt damp and unwelcoming and I crawled straight out again. Things would have to be very bad for me to venture in there voluntarily again.

But twelve hours later, that's exactly where I was – and nobody had to ask me twice.

The air-raid siren when it started was like the sound of your mum crying. It was an up-and-down wail and incredibly loud but it was what it stood for that cut right through your ears to your heart in one second. Being woken by that sound was the worst experience in the world because it wasn't an alarm clock, it was a warning. The Nazis were coming. Coming for us, coming for me.

It shook me up inside and I realised I was scared. More than scared, petrified, terrified, my hands were actually trembling as I clung on to the bed clothes. Then Dad appeared in the doorway.

'Come on, Boy-Boy, time to get in the shelter.'

'I don't want to go, Dad.'

'Don't be silly. Bring your blanket and your pillow with you if you want. Just hurry.'

That wasn't all I had to pick up. Next to the bed was my gas mask, my ration book, a change of clothes and a torch, all neatly arranged in a pile. Mum had done it for all of us in case of exactly this.

We all packed ourselves into the back of the hut, the part buried deepest under the earth. We wouldn't survive a direct hit in there but we should escape any collateral damage from falling bricks or debris if the houses were hit.

All the while we were silent. There was no point speaking, the siren was still too loud. Next door I could hear chattering coming from their steel shelter. That family hadn't been away like us. This wasn't the first time they'd heard the siren. That was the first clue I had that it wasn't the end of the world. Or at least it didn't have to be. People did survive bombing raids. The question was, would I?

Eventually we heard them. One Messerschmitt above Kent had been loud. By the sound of the mechanical thunder rolling towards us there could be as many as twenty or thirty planes and, from the way the noise was getting louder, they weren't even over our heads yet.

'Can I have a look, Dad?'

He shrugged. 'Two seconds.' Then to everyone else, he said, 'Nobody turn their torches on.'

I crawled over to the door and felt my brothers and sisters inches behind me.

'Just a crack,' Dad called out.

Nodding, I leaned my shoulder against the metal and felt it give. When it was enough for my head I stopped and looked up. It wasn't a clear sky but I could make out the moon to the east. And then, suddenly, it just disappeared. In its place was a swarm of black shapes, like locusts. It had been dark already. Now I couldn't see a thing.

I slammed the door shut and hurried back to my parents.

'They're here,' I said. I closed my eyes and waited.

Above the din of the siren and the wall of noise I could make out a single engine. One plane had to be closer to us than the others. I found myself concentrating on it, as though that would do something. Out of the buzzing fury I could soon make out another noise, like a whistle. It was high pitched and in its own way terrifying. Dad heard it too. Judging by his grimace, not for the first time.

'Brace yourselves,' he said.

A few seconds later the whistling stopped. I went to speak but the silence was shattered by a blast. The whistle had been a bomb falling and the quiet had been that split second between landing and detonation. The air-raid siren fell silent, or so it seemed as the explosion filled my ears. As they cleared I could make out a dull thumping in my head.

As the night went on, I experienced the same sensation again

and again. The buzzing, the whistling and the terrible power of
the bomb going off. I learned to hate that tiny space between the
whistling stopping and the blast. It was barely a second but it
seemed like a lifetime. You knew that the moment the whistling
ended, there was time for a heartbeat and then people were going
to die.

How long before it was us?

Above the noise I tried to work out whether each explosion
was closer or further away than the last one. The louder it was,
the closer the Luftwaffe were getting. If they started to fade we
could breathe a sigh of relief for a few minutes, maybe even for
the night. It was like seeing lightning then counting the seconds
until the roar of thunder to work out how close the storm is.
Maybe, I wondered, that's why they called this the Blitz (from the
German for lightning).

It was all I could do to avoid screaming while the bombard-
ment rained down nearby. It didn't matter how hard I pressed my
ears, I could still hear the whistles and the silences that followed.
Then I thought of Kitty. What must she and all the other animals
in the area be going through? Even Billy the goat didn't deserve
this. At least I knew what was causing the noise. On the other
hand, I also knew I could be blown up any minute. Was that
better than being ignorant like a goat? All I knew for sure was
that I'd have to check on them first thing.

The bomb with our name on it didn't come, not that night.
Nor the night after or the night after that. But for a week, two
weeks, three weeks, we found ourselves running out to the yard
in the dead of night, scrabbling over each other to get in and slam

the door just to keep the damned air-raid siren out. After so many days of alarms we were scared but we were tired, too. I realised I could sleep, even with bombers nearby. We all could. Even Dad managed to get forty winks when he wasn't on duty himself.

The constant upheaval affected people in different ways. Some families chose to go straight outside instead of bothering with bed. That way there was no panic later on. Mum said we could do that if we wanted and so when it wasn't too cold, we did. What she wouldn't do was agree to what our next-door neighbours opted for. After two months of disruption the husband and wife and their family just refused to go outside at all during the sirens.

'If your time's up, your time's up,' the old man said. 'And if I'm going to go, I want to be in my own bed.'

He wasn't the only person who thought like that. As soon as morning came round, the streets were full of kids trying to track down where the bombs had landed. If we treated it like a game it's because we had to. Everyone needed an outlet after the tension and fear during the hours of darkness. We were so young we found our fun where we could.

Of course, our smiles vanished entirely when we discovered what we were looking for.

Usually if there'd been a direct hit you could see the smoke, so we'd chase that down. Outside where a house used to be there'd be a crowd around a fire cart and a team from the station trying to extinguish the flames, so rescuers could get through the rubble to check for survivors. The first time I saw a bombed building I was nearly sick on the spot. The houses on that street looked the same as ours. The people who'd lived there were just like us. The only difference was, we'd used our shelter that night.

And they hadn't.

I don't know how long I stood there watching. I do know that when I heard one of the men in hard hats call out that he'd found someone my heart leaped. When I saw him shake his head a few seconds later I turned around. It was time to go. Hitler had made his point.

Maybe I was better off in Wales?

15

I Think It's a Bomb

I was born on Bridgeway Street in the house opposite where the pile of rubble now stood. A few weeks later I found myself staring at the hole on Chalton Street where three houses used to stand. The next night another one had gone, down the other end. Ossulston Street, the potato depot, Phoenix Road, Hampstead Road, even the buildings opposite my old Catholic school, St Aloysius, they all took direct hits. The scariest was at the top of Chalton. A parachute mine was dropped in Oakley Square. It could have gone anywhere in the wind. It could have drifted in through my open window. We were only a couple of hundred yards away as the plane flies.

As we heard the bombs come down on Aldenham Street, the closest we'd ever been to a direct hit, I tried to calm my siblings by joking that the priests at St Aloysius were Hitler's target. But it was no laughing matter and the morning after I was as devastated as everyone else that another two families were homeless and another couple had lost their lives.

Fifty-six nights in a row the Luftwaffe bombed London. I was away for some of it but it didn't feel like I'd missed anything. After a while anything becomes normal. Scrubbing the back of the disgusting Mr Davies was normal once. Hiding out for your life in a hut in the garden seemed as natural as burping once you'd done it three weeks in a row.

Life, though, went on. To prove it, we moved house again, this time around the corner to Charrington Street. I don't know why we did it but I was relieved to see they had an Anderson shelter in place. I helped as little as I could with the house move. I could never see the point. I checked my bed was all right then made myself scarce. The shelter was my priority. We'd be spending so much time there I wanted to make sure it was comfy, like the last one.

I was still sent to school, although things were different. Half our class had been evacuated. Some of the teachers had gone as well. It was hard concentrating knowing that none of us might be there the next day. But that didn't work as an excuse for not doing homework. A clip round the ear in wartime hurts just as much as one dished up during peace.

At least our school stayed open. A lot of them were taken over and used as morgues or military bases. They launched barrage balloons out of the grounds of some of them in an attempt to drive the Luftwaffe too high to hit their targets.

Dad was working pretty much full time with the brigade out of Euston Road or wherever they needed able bodies. Casualties were high and wherever he went he knew he was replacing a fallen comrade.

Mum was working double shifts at the Tolmer and Granddad was having to drive out on Kitty to pick up fruit direct from the farms just to keep his stocks going. We were all doing the best we could but no one smiled any more, not like they used to.

Granddad decided that we needed a party.

'The Führer can bomb our houses but he's not stealing Christmas!' he declared. The whole family was invited, as usual, to No. 151 on 25 December and we had the best party we could. But things weren't right. It was the first year there was no fruit on Granddad's ceiling. Even the paper chains looked less ambitious than usual. We'd made them out of old blackout and gas-mask posters dumped by the bins last year. That was a mistake. Every time I looked up through the tobacco smoke I could see reminders of what was going on out there in the real world.

We would get a reminder of that soon enough, we were sure of that. The air-raid siren would be going off any minute and that would be Christmas over for another year. At ten o'clock Uncle Patsy took a break from his piano playing and Granddad turned on his Cossor radio. The news came crackling through. In those days, everything was news. We had it on in the background for about an hour but, as gradually the talking got louder and more animated, we finally had to admit.

'They're not coming,' Granddad said. 'I think even Jerry wants to be at home for Christmas.'

Nervous laughter filled the room. Was Granddad right? Weren't they going to bomb us at Christmas? I thought of the face of the Messerschmitt pilot and how normal he looked. Maybe they're really not monsters.

The respite didn't last long. On Boxing Day the Moaning Minnie sirens droned into life once again and we rushed to the shelters. Mum had fixed a couple of strings of paper chains throughout the length of the hut. I wished Marjorie could be there to see it. Knowing she was out there somewhere, not wanting to come home, still made me feel sick. It was worse, in a way, than having Rags taken from me because my sister had chosen not to come back.

As the droning was drowned out by the hornet engines of the Heinkels on their way over, my thoughts shifted to the skies above and we all fell silent. Normal service had been resumed.

In fact, while the planes continued coming, something had changed over Christmas. We were used to hearing the explosions from the bombs. As one distant crack landed after another, I realised the noise was different. Whatever the Nazis were dropping now, it wasn't anything we'd had before.

The news was full of it the next day. Incendiary bombs, the experts called them. Whereas the high-explosive bombs could destroy a building in the blink of an eye, these devices could burn at 2,500 degrees C. Anything in their path would catch alight. The intention was clear. If Hitler couldn't raze us to the ground, he was going to burn us instead.

A couple of days later he went for it. I know, because we didn't see Dad for days. The Second Great Fire of London, the news called it. Two nights of saturation bombing, blanket coverage of the centre of town. There were so many incendiaries that the fire of one would link up with another. The War Office ordered for buildings like St Paul's Cathedral to be protected at all costs but,

Dad said, the truth was the whole city was in danger of going up. Getting the water out of the Thames wasn't helped by the low tide when the bombers unloaded. A major water pipe was also damaged and exploded during the operation.

Dad was on duty up at Hampstead one of these nights. An incendiary had set off one of the maple trees on the High Street. This had spread to all the others, like a bushfire in suburbia. A lot of the trees' branches touched the houses and shops on the pavement side, so protecting those was the priority. All the while, the bombs kept fizzing down. Dad wasn't far from the jewellers when it suddenly exploded. The front glass shattered into a million pieces and suddenly the night sky was filled with diamonds and rings and jewels flying through the air, twinkling in the reflection of the fire. Anyone brave enough to venture out of their shelters first would have struck gold.

The only good thing about the incendiaries was they didn't always go off. Usually that's when Dad and his buddies would be called out. But not always, we learned the hard way.

It was another morning after the night before. Chalton Street was just coming to life with the costers and the horses and carts. Down the bottom of the street you could see the cars and buses inching their way along the Euston Road. But that wasn't what Wally and I were looking at. We were staring at the reddish, round-headed thing in the gravel outside the Coffee House pub. It looked like a baseball bat or a policeman's metal truncheon, not much longer but maybe thicker.

'What is it, Boy-Boy?'

'I think it's a bomb,' I said. 'An incendiary, I suppose.'

'Why hasn't it gone off?'

'I don't know. Maybe it's dead.'

What we should have done was go back and find Dad. Or at least bang on the Coffee House door to get them all out. Instead we started throwing stones at it. Then, when that stopped being funny, Wally picked up a metal dustbin lid.

'Shall I?' he asked, his little face shining.

'Yeah!'

The lid was half my brother's size but he managed to get it a fair way. When it stopped short of the target, though, he just laughed and ran over to get it. I didn't think of stopping him, not even when he picked up the lid and smashed it down on the incendiary. But out of sight is out of mind. With the bomb covered once and for all, we decided to hunt out others. We'd barely got thirty feet when there was a crack like lightning – and the dustbin lid flew over our heads into the wall of the house opposite.

We hit the deck like we'd been shot. Slowly, I dared to look back. The incendiary had gone off and, because it was in the middle of the street, was burning itself out. The dustbin lid had soaked up most of the fury of the explosion but it had nearly killed us in the process.

That wasn't our only brush with them. I don't remember if we were slow to get down to the hut or if we were too bored of it to move. But I remember waking up to the sound of the air-raid siren and then diving under my bedclothes as the roof of the house tore apart. We all heard it. Something had come through the roof.

But there was no explosion.

'Get out!' Dad roared, and started dragging everyone out of their beds and over to the stairs. But while he dealt with Wally and the others I stood staring in his doorway. An incendiary bomb, just like the one we'd found on the street, was lying square in the middle of Mum and Dad's bed. If it had gone off they'd have been cooked in an instant.

Dad came rushing back in and went over to the window, tearing open the shutters and sash windows the second he could reach them. Then he took a huge breath and grabbed hold of the incendiary and chucked it out of the house.

Dad had checked that no one was in the street – he knew from experience that the incendiaries are dangerous if you're too close but safe enough in open spaces, but there'd been no time to warn anyone. I heard a lot of explosions when I was a kid, but that bang will live with me forever. It echoed up and down Charrington Street for minutes. Each echo shouted, 'That should have been you, Doles, that should have been you!'

I was lucky Dad was there. Most of the time he wasn't. Luckily I had other members of my family.

One Saturday evening we tried to pretend it was business as usual. Granddad and I went out on a tour of the beer houses with our collection jars. Times were tough for everyone but there were always people worse off. If you can afford a few pence for a beer, he said, think of those poor beggars who can't.

We were doing okay, filling our tins nicely, and were on our way up Eversholt Street when the sirens went off. I could see Granddad thinking. How long did we have before the planes were overhead? If he'd been on his own I'm pretty sure he would have run for home. But he had me to look after. He didn't want to answer to Mary Dole about why he kept her boy out during a raid.

'Quick,' he said eventually, 'into the station.'

I was surprised to see so many others running in the same direction. Euston was a huge target. One bomb in the right place and it could come down on all our heads. Why did Granddad think we would be safe there?

But we never got as far as the concourse. No one did. Everyone was filing down the steps to the Underground. We joined the back of the queue and followed the line. Most people had blankets and pillows. A lot of the kids were carrying soft toys. They'd all done this before.

Even before we'd reached the bottom of the stairs, both receiving a few slaps on the back courtesy of our suits along the way, I wondered where everyone was going. There couldn't be any trains running. And where would they go? When the crowd spilled out onto the platform and I saw hundreds of people already in place for the night, I couldn't believe it. Some of them looked like they'd been down there for days, weeks. They had little windbreaks marking off their territory, and pots and pans of water and tins of food. They were asking the newcomers what it was like 'up there'.

Granddad shook his head. 'They mean on the surface,' he explained. 'These are the people the government was worried about.'

'Who?'

'The ones who are hiding out down here. Mr Churchill doesn't want people living underground. He doesn't want Hitler to think we're scared.'

'I'm not,' I said.

'I know, sonny. Stiff upper lip, eh?'

The deeper we went, the quieter the sirens. I'd never heard them so muffled but then I'd never been 150 feet underground while they were sounding off. I wondered why we didn't come down here more often.

We picked our way over the legs of those already comfortable until we found a space. As we went to sit down a voice called out.

'Look, it's a Pearly. Give us a song, would you?'

Granddad raised his hand to say sorry, but no, and continued to sit down. But the guy wouldn't pipe down and when he said it again a load of other people saw who he was talking to.

'Hey, it's George, the Pearly King of St Pancras,' another one said. 'And who's he got with him? Are you a Pearly as well, son?'

I looked at Granddad for help. He smiled and nodded.

'Yes, I am,' I said. 'I'm the Pearly Prince of St Pancras – and one day I'll be King like my granddad.'

Granddad laughed. 'Hopefully I've got a few good years in me yet.' As another call came for him to give everyone on Platform 2 a song, he rose to his feet.

'Well, young Alfie,' he said to me, puffing his chest out to its fullest, 'it looks to me like we've got ourselves a captive audience. So let's see what we can do to raise a smile down here.'

And off he went. A story, a joke and a song. I joined in and did a little dance while the people around us clapped. Some of the other kids who'd looked scared a few minutes earlier edged over and began to join in. Even as the sound of incendiaries fizzing and cracking into life far above our heads continued, all eyes and ears were on us. I'd always been proud to be a Pearly but that night was special. We raised money but more than that we raised spirits. For a short while no one thought about the death and poverty at ground level. We all had a laugh and no one felt guilty for hiding from the bombs.

The Blitz ended as suddenly as it had begun in the summer of 1941. Hitler apparently had other fish to fry. For some people, however, the bombs never stopped falling. I was walking along the Euston Road one day and I heard a trolley bus backfire. A short way in front of me a man dived to the floor, his hands over his head.

'Get down!' he screamed. 'They're coming, get down!'

Even when an old man told him that it was an engine fault he couldn't be calmed. He was sobbing with fear.

'Shell shock', Dad called it. He'd seen plenty of them on his travels. People who were so scarred by hearing the bombs drop every night that they heard them whenever there was a loud noise. I saw it closer to home as well. A cousin of ours, Boysie Davies, suffered with the noises. I watched him lose the plot one day while he was walking past a bombsite that had been fenced off with barbed wire. The panic in his eyes was enough to scare anyone. I don't know what he could hear but he looked left, then he looked right, then he dived into the barbed wire screaming, 'They're coming! They're coming!' He tore himself to shreds and he never recovered, not in his head. The war for him was already over.

I hoped it would go better for the rest of us. Even without the nightly blanket bombing life just seemed to get harder and harder. Granddad was having to travel further and further afield to stock up his shop. He made it work to his advantage, becoming a wholesaler of sorts for the local costers. But it made him tired before a long day in the shop.

It was Uncle Patsy I felt most sorry for. With meat rations turning everyone into walking skeletons he knew he had the solution in his loft. When he finally offered a couple of pigeons up for a special family meal, we knew how much it hurt him. The war made us all do desperate things.

Not everyone came out of it smelling of roses. Mum let the top floor of the house to a vicar whose own place next to the church had been destroyed. He arrived with his son but I wish they hadn't. I used to hear that poor kid being made to recite passages from the Bible day and night. Even when he was in the outdoor lav he'd have to take his scriptures in with him. His dad would sometimes walk past the door and if he couldn't hear junior reading away there was a wallop waiting when he'd wiped his backside.

That's not what made me hate him, though. The church got a lot of charity help, including clothes and food, to distribute among the less well-off members of his congregation. The vicar pocketed a lot of it. If the clothes fit him or his boy, they had them. If the food was something they didn't have, it came home with them. Jam was his big weakness. A farmer sent jars of it every few weeks to be passed on as treats to his flock. Not one jar ever made it out of his clutches. I used to see him unpacking it from his vicar's smock when he got inside the front door. I wouldn't have minded so much if he'd offered me some, but he never did.

In September 1941 I moved schools. I was a senior now so it was time to mingle with the big boys. After years of watching the kids at Medburn Street School dangling their arms through the fences begging Granddad for an apple, I'd now be able to join them. Unfortunately, I knew Granddad wouldn't think twice about charging me as much as the next boy.

Maybe I should wait till I see Grandma walking by . . .

I didn't get on at senior school. The teachers were a bit too free with their fists for my liking. Besides, I didn't even want to be there. War or no war, I had a job to go to . . .

Hunger drove people to look for food everywhere. Someone told me that they had guards at Regent's Park Zoo in case anyone felt like hunting for their dinner. I never believed that, although I do know that a lot of the animals were evacuated out to Whipsnade in Bedfordshire, so maybe there was something in it. Whipsnade didn't have the facilities for poisonous snakes and bugs so they were all destroyed in case a bomb in the complex set them free. The last thing London needed on top of everything else was an outbreak of anaconda attacks.

I would have been one of the first casualties. I was spending so much time on the canal after school and at weekends that any predator could have picked me off. I wasn't alone, though. Whereas it used to be me dodging the waterways police for fishing without a licence, now it was so popular I was lucky to find a patch wide enough to spread my blanket to sit on.

Most people didn't go too far inside the park with their rods, though, so that's where I headed. The three-island pond was a different shape in the 1940s and there used to be a little inlet that I liked to hunker down in, as low in the reeds as I could get, away from the spying eyes of the park keepers and the boat owners. On a good day I'd land a couple of roach before I was told to sling my hook homewards. On a very good day I'd have enough to feed the five thousand.

Maybe one or two we'd coat in salt and try to keep fresh for a few days. But we didn't have freezers and I didn't want to waste what I caught, so I took a leaf out of Granddad's book and started hawking my wares around the park. It took me about a minute to find a buyer. A Jewish fella was walking with his wife.

'What have you got, boy?'

It was almost like he knew my name.

'A couple of roach for sale, sir. Would you like 'em?'

'I'll tell you what. Bring them to my house and if I like them I'll buy two off you every day.'

'Deal.'

He lived with his family in a block of flats around the east side of the park called The White House. It's a hotel now. I got a few looks from the neighbours who didn't appreciate the pong when I went in, but that was a nice little earner for me. When someone else tried to buy one off me, my customer heard about it and got angry. I could do what I wanted, he said, as long as I delivered to him first. If I missed a day, the deal was off.

Not everyone wanted food every day. The money I got for the fish helped Mum out buying our share of rationed meat – when the butcher had any. Some days there would be bugger all behind the counter, not even the horse meat that most of them had started selling. Personally I couldn't eat it. It would have been like eating Kitty. But Mum smuggled it into stews without telling me, so I suppose it tasted okay.

When a delivery lorry was spotted outside the butcher's shop, word would go round and you'd have a queue outside within minutes. When he was due a shipment Mum used to keep one of us on 'meat watch'.

'He's had nothing for two days so it's about time. If you see a van outside his shop, you get in the queue and tell someone to fetch me for the book.'

It usually worked out okay unless the can I was kicking went round the corner and I chased it, forgetting where I was meant to be playing. Once I walked back towards the butchers and saw there were already forty people snaking down the street.

'Bloomin' 'ell, Mum's gonna kill me!'

Luckily I saw one of my aunts, Polly, up the front. I shot home, grabbed our books and tore back, begging her to pick up our four rashers of bacon each and whatever other cuts of pork we were allowed.

Everything was getting tighter. Eggs were few and far between so the shops started selling dried egg powder. It was all right for scrambled but if you wanted egg and soldiers you were unlucky.

There was a lot of talk about alternatives, especially to sugar and flour. Carrots featured in virtually everything, from roasts to cakes. Potatoes were also pretty easy to find. Getting the oil to make chips was the hardest thing. At some point the store began stocking tinned meats. The ration system was changed to a points system so you could stock up on things that were available rather than stuff that was not. When Mum saw a stack of spam or corned beef from America she bought as many as she was allowed. When we were hopping one year Dad got a bit more adventurous with our vouchers and turned up one Friday night with five tins of casserole – made from whale meat.

'Horses are one thing, but what do you expect me to do with that?' Mum said.

'I don't know. Just cook it and see what it tastes like. The poster said it's like meat and fish all at once.'

Mum wasn't so sure, but with Dad standing over her she picked up the tins and put them on the fire.

'You'd better be hungry, Alfie Dole.'

Her next job was to track us down to eat. By the time I started wandering back over the common from the pond I heard a bang, like a gun shot, then something breaking, then swearing, all in the space of two seconds. I ran towards the fire.

'Stay back, Boy-Boy!' Dad called out, desperately trying to hook something out of the fire with a stick. 'It's a war zone here.'

I couldn't help laughing. He was covered in brown paste. Behind him, the nearest hut had a cracked window. One of the whale-meat tins, he said, had exploded in the heat. He was trying to fish the others out before they went off as well.

Of course, he laughed about it later. Or Mum did, anyway.

'Typical Alfie Dole,' she said, regaling everyone around the fire, 'he manages to escape an incendiary on his own bed then gets himself shot by whale meat.'

Not much changed on our hopping trips, but food was the centre of everything we did. As soon as we arrived at Bore Green, a farmer from next door came over with an offer. Save all your vegetable scraps for my pigs, he said, and when one's ready for the slaughter you'll get a share. On top of the ration book amount, this was too good to turn down. Everyone joined in. By the time we were getting to the end of our stay, Mum got a bit anxious and went to find the farmer, with me tagging along behind. She needn't have worried. He took us into a barn and showed us two porkers hanging down from hooks, blood dripping down their sides.

'I'll see you Sunday,' he said.

Back home there were similar trades being made wherever there was a bit of green space. People had pigs, goats, rabbits, poultry – anything they could plump up then have for dinner. If you helped feed them you might be promised a thigh or a breast.

We didn't have any animals, apart from Patsy's pigeons and Granddad's goat, Billy, but we had a bit of mud. Neville Chamberlain's 'Dig For Victory' posters were all over the place encouraging you to plant some veg if you had the land, so we had carrots, of course, and spuds and runner beans and a couple of rows of cabbages in our yard. We even had parsnips coming out of the roof of the Anderson. Come summer the whole shelter was camouflaged.

More people growing their own should have been a problem for Granddad but, the truth was, he was finding it hard to keep his own stocks sufficient enough to meet demand. When he did manage to get a crate of oranges in, he put a sign on them saying,

'Children only'. It wasn't the time to get fussy about the quality, either. We were all 'Speckys' now.

Some things I didn't realise had faded from our lives completely. It was only when I described the moon as banana-shaped and Peter said, 'What does that mean?' that I realised he couldn't remember seeing one – and I didn't know when that would ever change. Then one day I pushed Granddad's barrow for him down to York Way and there they were, coming off a train, stacks and stacks of boxes that looked like coffins, all containing bright-green bananas. Men were carrying the caskets over to a warehouse and breaking them open and hanging the stalks in big clumps from hooks. Then they were flogging them, a hand at a time. Even though he was in the trade, Granddad was limited to what he could take.

When the rationing came in I was nine and it didn't register. Meals weren't that special beforehand. By the time I was twelve it was affecting every aspect of my life. Lack of petrol and diesel meant we had to get all our furniture and luggage down to Paddock Wood by train or horse. Things like soap became scarce, not that that bothered me so much. The worst thing was clothes. Everyone had a certain amount of units to last a year. Adults got sixty-six, kids got more because we were expected to outgrow things. Sometimes you'd have to make stuff out of old fabrics, wherever you found them. You could spot the kid who was dressed in curtains dug out of the rubble of someone else's place. When the barrage balloons came down in the park they'd get cut up and made into raincoats or hats. Difficulties getting hold of elastic meant it was hard to even adapt what you did have.

Worst of all, because of the shortage of cotton, kids were banned from wearing long trousers until the age of twelve.

I couldn't wait for the day to come. Not because my legs were getting cold or because I'd outgrown my shorts. I needed long trousers because I'd discovered girls. If I was going to act like a man, I needed to look like one, too.

16

This is My Stop

I wondered sometimes if the men left behind during the war felt they had a point to prove. Dad was in his forties but he still risked his life, especially during the Blitz, putting out fires all over Camden. Without men like him, we'd have been toast. Half the London skyline as we know it today wouldn't be there any more. Teachers, though? Did we really need them? The more I turned up to school, the more I found myself thinking that.

The ones that hadn't been evacuated didn't look like they enjoyed being there any more than I did. One word out of turn and I got a blackboard rubber thrown at my head. And if it hit the kid behind me the teacher, Mr Malcolm, didn't care. He'd got it out of his system, whatever 'it' was. The school was full of men like that, men who threw their weight around because they could. They'd flick your ears in passing, tug the sideburns of the older boys or kick you in the spine when you were sitting on the floor in assembly. To me, it was bullying, plain and simple. If they'd carried on like that on the streets people like my dad would have put them straight. Put them on their backs. Put them in an ambulance. Take your pick.

It wasn't just my school where there was a problem – and it wasn't just Dad who wouldn't be happy about it. Wally came home one day afraid to let Mum see him. After he'd sat through tea without once moving his hand from his cheek, she smelled a rat.

'Let me see your face.'

He hesitated, then gave in. He had a shiner just below his eye.

'Have you been fighting?'

'No!' The way he shot his answer back told us all he wasn't lying. I could see Mum's brain ticking.

'Did Mr Williams do this to you?'

Nothing. Wally wouldn't reply. It was one thing getting hit by your teacher, it was another grassing him up. Who knew what the punishment for that would be?

'Get your coat, Walter. I'm going to have a word with him.'

With my brother begging her not to go, clinging round her waist to stop her, Mum stormed out of the door and towards the school, muttering to herself all the way.

'Hitting a six-year-old, indeed. Who does he think he is?'

Some people would have cooled down by the time they'd walked at speed for five minutes. Not Mum. We just turned the corner in time to see her punch the door knocker at the main entrance before barging the door open. We caught up as the headmaster confronted her.

'Is there a problem, Mrs Dole?'

'Where's Williams?' Mum said, marching past him.

A strong head would have handled the situation on his colleague's behalf. This one pointed to a staircase then fled in the opposite direction.

Mr Williams was a big man, an ex-rugby player, a drinker and a smoker. He was puffing on his pipe at his desk when Mum led us into the room. Before he could say a word, she'd slapped him round the face, good and proper.

'Think it's all right to hit young lads, do you? How do you like it?'

She raised her arm again but this time he caught it. He was old but not slow. And not stupid, either. He sensed immediately what he was up against and didn't fancy his odds.

'I don't know what Walter told you but it was just an accident,' he said. He went on to say that Wally had been messing around by the window. Wally blushed. This much was obviously true. I found it hard not to laugh at my naughty brother messing around while this clown's back was turned. But, whatever Williams said, Wally had clearly been rumbled and been made to pay for it.

Mum had come to the same conclusion. She let him have both barrels until he swore he wouldn't hit anyone again.

'You shouldn't be allowed near kids, you're an animal.'

As we left the room I couldn't resist sticking my tongue out. He wasn't my teacher, what could he do to me? His last words were, 'Who put you in charge, you bloody Nazi?' Unfortunately for him, Mum heard.

'What did you say?' She looked menacing with her hands on her hips.

'Nothing,' Williams mumbled.

I thought it was over but now Mum had to find the head and tell him what he should be doing. The next week Williams was moved away from the class.

Mum never had it out with any of my teachers like that but then I didn't give them as much trouble – mainly because I was hardly there. I decided pretty early on that school wasn't for me. Books couldn't beat fishing for a living. In any case, as soon as I was old enough I'd be conscripted. The news was telling us every night how many men were dying in Europe or at sea. What was the point in wasting the only years I had left before I was sent to be shot at by Hitler?

But Medburn Street did have its advantages. One was that it gave me a free lunch. That saved a ticket or two from the ration book. Even on days when I bunked off to go scrumping or fishing, I often called back in time to get a plate of whatever they'd managed to conjure out of the limited stock.

The other advantage to school was girls. There were lots of them and one or two of them seemed to think I was pretty nice. That was all the persuasion I needed to hang around. They'd giggle in the classroom when I was a bit cheeky and hang around the playground until I came out for break. Conversation was a bit stilted so I'd act the clown. I'd had enough tough crowds as a Pearly and these girls liked me to start with so it shouldn't have been too hard.

Some of my mates tagged along for the ride. They didn't know what was going to come of me being so close to girls but it had to be better than them trying to chat them up. It was unlikely but maybe I would even get one of the girls to go out on a date with me, then the girl's friends and mine could go out together as well. Not all boys, sadly, were that mature.

'Well, if it isn't his royal bleedin' highness,' one called out. 'Are you going to give 'em a little dance as well?'

'Of course, he's not,' another one chipped in. 'He's nothing without his granddad. He's just the monkey.'

I decided to ignore them. Fighting in the playground would just get me into more trouble than usual. Then one of them said, 'Where's your girly little suit now? Is it at home with your dolls?'

Enough was enough. Hit the biggest, hit them first and hit them hard. My dad's advice rang in my ears as I punched the tallest boy in the stomach. He went to fight back but his mates had bombed off so he decided to follow them, swearing threat after threat back at me as he fled. I was out of breath and I'd barely moved. *Nobody insults the good Pearly name,* I thought. But that wasn't the only reason I was gasping for air. One of the girls had just put her hand into mine.

I had a smile on my face for the rest of the day.

Impressing girls when you've got no money is hard. The only positive was that they had no money either. No one did. The fact I was even trying was enough to please a pretty blonde girl called June. She wasn't the prettiest of the three girls who had taken a shine to me but her giggle was infectious and she was the quickest with a cheeky reply after I'd said something.

My easy-come-easy-go approach to attendance did a lot of the work for me. Even when I hadn't shown up for lessons, June knew I'd be hanging around the gates come four o'clock. If I had a Fyffes banana from No. 151, all the better. Her mum was like mine; happy enough whatever we did as long as she knew where we were doing it, so when I said, 'Let's go up to Hampstead Heath,' June was up for it, even though it was a fair walk.

'Be back before dark,' her mum said. 'And if you lose your bearings, just follow the tram tracks home.'

It was good advice. They ran down Hampstead High Street, through Belsize Park, Chalk Farm and Camden High Street to Mornington Crescent and home.

Going out together was one thing but basically we were just mates. June and I did the same stuff that I was doing with my other muckers. We ran, hid, kicked stones, annoyed shopkeepers and generally laughed until we dropped. I even took her fishing. She didn't like pinning the worm on the hook but she was happy enough to sit there while I dropped a line.

As time went by and June became Joan who became Gwen who became Sally, I realised there were differences between girls and my mates. With my friends and brothers I'd do stupid things for a dare. But where Sally and the others were concerned I was going all out to impress. We were down Gray's Inn Road one day, walking back from the river. Sally was tired.

'Let's get a ride,' I suggested, watching the trams and trolley buses inching along beside us.

'I haven't got any money.'

That was a problem. Neither had I. Normally I'd have left it there. But I was with Sally. I didn't know how long for, but I was damned sure I was going to pull out the stops while I was.

'Who needs money?' I said, and ran towards a taxi stuck in the traffic. Like all the cars at the time, it had a high, almost vertical back. There was a thick bumper running along the bottom and a spare wheel stuck to the back. It was almost as though the driver wanted us to climb on board.

I ducked under the back window and clambered onto the bumper.

'Come on!' I called out.

For a moment Sally looked horrified. Then she giggled and ran over to join me.

When the taxi pulled away her face changed again. I wasn't sure she could hang on tight enough and neither was she. But gradually she relaxed. In fact, she even blew a kiss to the car tooting its horn behind.

We joined the Euston Road and that's when the driver put his foot down. I knew it wouldn't last. There were too many buses. We were at Tolmer's Square when it slowed to a halt.

'This is my stop,' I said, laughing, and hopped off. For a second I thought Sally was staying on because she was too nervous to let go in case the cab pulled away, but she jumped down and called out 'Thanks' to the confused driver who wondered where we'd suddenly come from.

Being able to take a friend into the tuppenny rush for less than tuppence stood me in good stead as well. When Mum left the Tolmer to work at the Carreras cigarette factory on Hampstead Road I felt let down. Typical kid-in-love logic – she only left because the Tolmer had been bombed.

The only other thing I could show off was my Pearly suit. By the time I was thirteen I was on my third version. Funnily enough, pulling it on in front of a girl didn't make me feel as good as I'd hoped. I felt odd, self-conscious. Was I actually embarrassed to be wearing it? Whatever the feeling was, I didn't like it, so I decided never to let a girl see me in it again. A few days later, Sally said, 'My dad saw you in the Coffee House with your granddad. He said he was proud of you.' As she spoke, Sally looked proud as well, but was she mocking me really?

'That's girls for you,' Mum said. That made me even more confused. Wasn't she a girl as well?

Between fishing for the family and the Jewish lot, chasing girls and making the occasional appearance at school, I didn't have much time left over. When Granddad said there was a temporary space for a porter at Covent Garden, though, I decided to do it. The hours were weekends and before school. I expected Mum to say no but she just asked me how much I'd be getting paid.

'Fifteen shillings a week,' I said.

'Well, you can give me ten of those for your board.'

'Okay.'

And that was it, I was working.

A lot of the wholesalers knew me on sight and it didn't take long for the traders and everyone else to learn that I was Specky Dole's boy. Everyone had a good word for Granddad. There's only so far that goodwill will get you, though. It was as much use as a chocolate fireguard when it came to lugging the crates and sacks around. Everyone was in such a hurry as well, I didn't get a breather until gone eight. Then I realised it was time to leg it up the hill to school.

By the time the position at the market finished I was hooked on getting a wage. I couldn't wait to leave school and start earning properly. I managed to last until I was fourteen but, in truth, I'd stopped going regularly long before that.

Because I loved animals so much, I got a job with a vet on Royal College Street, next door to the training college, but I didn't last long. Not many people had the money for vets during the war and the ones that did upset me with their burned puppies or lame horses. I don't know how doctors and nurses do it, let alone the vet. Seeing an animal in distress really turned my stomach.

Horses were working more than ever during the war. As petrol was rationed, even those with cars and vans turned back to single horse power. With so many out there every day it was a shame that one of the smaller casualties of the war was the cancellation of the Whitsun parade for working animals. In true Pearly spirit, Granddad reckoned it would give Londoners something to smile about if they brought it back, but the powers that be didn't agree. So much for not letting our way of life be disrupted by the Nazis.

I was even sadder when I got a new job because I would actually have been eligible to compete against Granddad and Kitty – I'd have loved to have seen their faces. It started when I asked the stationmaster down at Euston if there were any jobs going. He looked me up and down, thought about it a bit, then said, 'Are you any good with animals?'

I grinned. I liked the job already.

The next morning I was round the sidings where the mail train came in, heaving sacks of clothes and coats onto a cart. All the posh shops in Savile Row or Jermyn Street in Piccadilly and the West End ordered their stock from warehouses in the Midlands or further afield, then it was brought down by train and a driver on a cart drove round making deliveries. Even with the rationing on fabrics, those with money found a way to spend it. A suit from Savile Row cost the same as a week or even a month's rent for most people, and anyone who watched the shops knew what the cart was carrying. So that's where I came in. I was a driver's mate, there to guard the cargo and make sure the horse didn't go wandering off while the driver made his drop. I wasn't sure about being a guard, but minding the horse sounded fun; not like work at all.

Harold was the name of the fella I hopped up next to. Or Mr Smith, as he liked me to call him. He wasn't one for talking, as we trotted down to the West End, but every so often we'd go past a spot where a building used to be and he'd take his hat off as a show of respect for whoever had lived there.

His horse was Rita. She was a proper plodder, mooching up and down streets like she'd seen them all once too many times before. That was all for show. The second Harold stepped out of sight, she'd pull away. I'd driven Kitty enough to know my way around the reins but this Rita was on a different page. By the time Mr Smith came back out Rita and I were fifty yards up the Row.

I told him that Rita had dragged us away but he wouldn't have it. At the next drop-off he tied her to a lamppost and told me to stay off the cart.

It didn't matter how many times I was left on the seat, Rita would try to move off. If I found a bit of sugar she'd stop but the second it was gone, she was stomping to get going. The second Harold appeared, she was as good as gold.

'This isn't working out, lad,' he said, after another walk up the street to find us. 'We'll finish today then that's it.'

Now it was my turn to ride in silence for the last three drop-offs. We were heading round to Covent Garden via Oxford Street and, unusually, there were still quite a few packages on the flatbed behind me. When Mr Smith hopped off with two of them he didn't bother to tie us up.

'I'll be back before you've time to cause trouble,' he grumbled.

It turned out he wasn't. I think we must have been followed. Mr Smith had just set foot inside the tailor's when I heard men's voices just over my shoulder. Two fellas on another cart were leaning across to half-inch our packages. When I called out for them to stop they just laughed.

Right, I thought, come on, Rita.

I lifted the reins up and smacked them down on Rita's backside with all my strength. She wasn't expecting it. Neither were the blokes behind me. One of them was already on our cart, but not for long. Rita bolted forwards like she'd been fired out of a cannon and the thief flew backwards, onto his bum then over the side. The parcel he was holding cushioned his fall. Before he could get up, Mr Smith was standing over him with an expression on his face that I will never forget. He helped the guy to his feet then punched him square in the face until he fell back down. Then he did it again and again until the fella's oppo appeared to drag him away, begging for mercy.

I watched all this from a hundred yards away where Rita had finally stopped. Who knew that quiet Mr Smith, old Harold who cried for people he didn't know, had it in him?

After that he said I could keep my job, but I never got the hang of Rita so in the end I left before he could fire me again. I had another job to go to – and this time I'd been headhunted for a very important role.

'I'm sorry, Mr Smith,' I said, as I resigned. 'But the country needs me.'

I was exaggerating about my country needing me but for my brother David it was true. His conscription letter had arrived and we all had to come to terms with him being sent off to Aldershot to train for combat. He would be there for a few months and then no one knew what would happen. We all prayed he'd be found something in London but everyone knew a family with a young man overseas, many in Africa. Still, as we said goodbye to David at Waterloo, no one mentioned that. It was best for everyone if we pretended everything was going to be all right.

Two months later, on 6 June 1944, the whole family was huddled round Granddad's Cossor valve radio. The Allied Forces had landed in Normandy – D-Day, it became known as. For all of us, there was the sense that this was the beginning of the end. The Luftwaffe hadn't broken our air and sea defences and now British troops were marching on Occupied French soil while Germany concentrated on the other side of Europe.

Churchill's government, however, was not so quick to celebrate. Warnings were issued about imminent rocket attacks on

England. We were to be ready to retreat to our bunkers once again. Ours hadn't been touched for months except as a hidey-hole for Wally, Pete and their friends. Getting in there now posed a problem, as we were all that much bigger, and not just us kids. Mum was pregnant again.

'The Dole record of seventeen could yet be broken,' Dad joked.

'Not if I have a say in it, it won't,' Mum replied.

As in most things, sadly Churchill was right. Stung when we went marching over there, Hitler's airborne retaliation came a week later. This time though, the Luftwaffe stayed at home. What we got instead was like something out of a science-fiction film at the Tolmer.

The V-1s were bombs like nothing we'd seen before. They were twenty-seven feet long, weighed two tons and had the blast power of a dozen of the ones that rained down during the Blitz. But that wasn't what scared the pants off you in your shelter. The thing about the V-1 was that it looked like a bomber plane but it had no pilot. In fact, it didn't even need to be fired in this country to hit us. Somewhere in France and Holland there were giant guns armed with these monsters and aimed straight at us.

On D-Day we didn't know that. Even when the first V-1s, or Doodlebugs as we called them, came over on the night of 13 June, wiping out parts of Mile End in the process, we thought it was the Heinkels dropping their load. Then there were reports that these bombers just fell out of the sky. No one believed it. What pilot would dive headfirst into a factory in the East End?

Then gradually we all saw them with our own eyes. They

were like ghost ships in the moonlight. They had their coordinates, they were launched and there was nothing we could do to stop them. At least with a pilot he could change his mind or the bomb hatch might jam. These V-1s were already up in the air. The only place they could go was down.

Over the next few days even more barrage balloons went up to try to set the bombs off in midair. The railway stations around us got their fair share of protection. The rest of Somers Town wasn't so well protected.

It had been a while since we'd heard the air-raid sirens. Apart from tests, they'd stayed silent for months. When they cranked up in June 1944 all the old memories and nightmares came back. My gas mask didn't fit me any more so I left it in the house. Then we went outside, buried ourselves in the shelter and tried to keep spirits up with a sing-song. Dad was on call, waiting to deal with the fallout. David was in the army himself. That left me to look after the others with Mum.

Once you've got over the fact that there are no pilots in the planes overhead, that's when the fear comes. The V-1s had engines that propelled themselves up. You could hear them fizzing, as vicious as anything from the Blitz. It was when the throttle was cut and the plane went silent that you felt the bile rise in your throat. This was it. The bomb was falling. And you had no idea where it was heading.

From June to October the V-1s, then V-2s, came down. Then in the morning we'd come blinking out of our shelters, the sirens still ringing in our ears long after they'd been switched off, and try to get on with our lives. That's what we'd always done.

That's what Churchill wanted us to do now. Mourn your dead, pray for loved ones, but get back to work, get back to living or the war is lost.

That was easier said than done when you were looking at a road filled with what used to be a row of houses and pockets of flames being brought under control by Dad and his men. Sometimes the homes came down, leaving buildings either side. Seeing ruins on the ground was stomach-churning. Seeing half a bedroom, half a kitchen, half a front room, hanging in midair brought tears to all but the most hardened souls. Who'd been sleeping in that bed? Who was cooking at that stove? Who'd been in the bath by the fire? Hopefully no one. Hopefully the tenants were out the back in the shelter. But you just didn't know until the firemen put out the blazes and went through the bricks.

Getting things back to normal became a full-time job once more – for me as well.

Some of the buildings hit were complete write-offs and had to be demolished. When that happened I'd go through the rubble and pull out anything that looked like firewood. It was macabre but I wasn't the only one doing it. We couldn't afford enough coal when it got cold and if the next winter was going to be like the last, we needed to be stockpiling alternatives now.

Other buildings could be patched up. 'Make Do And Mend' was the phrase of the day. Builders, like my Uncle Patsy, worked nonstop to get rubble and ruins cleared and families back in their houses.

I saw a lot of Patsy and his clean-up crew in the weeks following D-Day. Everywhere you looked there were ladders up against buildings and men crawling over rooftops fixing chimneys or ripping off damaged slates and dragging tarpaulin over the holes. The richer buildings had proper scaffolding. One of the towers at the Houses of Parliament was covered in the metal the last time I'd been down that way.

In our area, though, we managed with ladders and good luck. But not every rooftop was accessible and plenty of them didn't look safe enough to take a heavy builder's weight, which is why Patsy asked if I fancied coming along to help out – and I did. This was what Mr Churchill would have wanted me to do. This was my chance to help repair the country.

Mum, though, was against it and even the money wouldn't make her reconsider.

'Look, Mary,' Dad said, 'Patsy knows that if anything happens to Boy-Boy he'll have me to answer to. Do you think he'd risk that?'

That was the clincher. Patsy was scared of 'Mad Alf' and always had been.

The work was fun. Dangerous, but fun. The first ladder I went up felt like it would fall over at any minute. Standing at the foot, Uncle Pat encouraged me to keep going and not look down. Of course, as soon as he said that I did. I couldn't help it. The next few seconds were spent hugging the wooden rungs for all I was worth.

'You'd better hurry before the wind picks up,' he called out.

The thought of being blown around was even more scary, so I sucked in a deep breath and ran up the rest of the way.

I froze again the minute I reached the top. The roof reached a point about six foot away from me, and around the perimeter there was a narrow gutter that you could just about walk along if you were careful. But that wasn't what caught my attention. Patsy hadn't told me about the view. We were round the back of St Pancras and I could see the barrage balloons over the Thames. Even as I clung on to the side of the gutter, I was thinking about bringing Carmen – Sally's successor – up there as soon as I could. Only a nail hitting the side of my head brought me out of my reverie.

'You'll get used to it,' a man called Bobby said. And to prove how used to it he was, he made a point of closing his eyes and running along the guttering. I was so scared he was going to fall but when he got to the other end and laughed at the look on my face I actually wished he had.

With the men standing on the relatively safe surface of the gutter, I was given a boost up by Bobby so I could crawl up the slates to the apex of the roof where there was a hole about three foot wide. It could have been weakened a year or two earlier but had got worse over winter. Some places just fell apart because of the fallout of the noise and vibrations of the bombs. Forget being a Pearly Prince, I felt like the King of London perched up there. I could see everywhere. It was even better than the view from Primrose Hill or Hampstead Heath because it felt like I was right in the centre of the city.

Patsy and his mates passed me up the boards to block the hole then when I'd got that in place they threw over the tarpaulin while I made sure the wood held underneath. It was hard work but exhilarating. When we'd finished I was sad to go back down.

Actually, I was more than sad. I was terrified. Climbing onto a ladder backwards three storeys high was ten times harder than going up. No one joked this time, not even Bobby. After my hard graft I think I'd earned that at least.

It didn't take long to feel part of the team. When Dad asked me how I was being treated I could honestly say I was fine. I got on with everyone. Once you prove your worth, in any job, you win respect.

I never got lazy though, or complacent. Uncle Patsy wouldn't let me. For someone who was used to launching pigeons into the air, he was surprisingly cagey about taking risks on a roof. He was the only one. Maybe that's why he survived.

Bobby, on the other hand, loved the roofs. 'Like being on top of the world,' he used to say. He took so many risks that made me feel sick but he was like a cat, sure-footed and good with his balance. He was lucky, too. Luck, however, has a way of deserting even its best friends.

We were working in Oakley Square, where the library is now. We'd nailed the tarpaulin down and were heading back for the ladder when Patsy noticed a corner of the sheet had somehow come loose. He went to go back when Bobby said, 'I'll do it, gaffer. It's my mistake.' He jogged along the gutter as normal, then almost vaulted over the pitched roof and down the other side just like he'd done dozens of times before. I heard him nailing the tarp down then saw his head as he stood back up. He gave me and Patsy a wink to say he'd done then, just as I put a foot on the top rung of the ladder, I heard a shout. When I looked back I saw a look on Bobby's face I'd never seen before:

Fear.

Then he disappeared off the back of the building.

Patsy wouldn't let me look but I found a way through the bodies standing round. Somewhere in that mess of bone, rags and blood was Bobby.

I knew then that that was my last day on the roofs. I didn't need to wait for Mum to tell me. Government orders or not, something had to change.

'I'm sorry, Mr Churchill,' I said. 'I can't just carry on as normal any more.'

17

We Won't Be Needing
These Any More

When the Blitz was raging, I was scared I was going to die. When the doodlebugs started showering down I was scared my family was. I was only fourteen but I got a glimpse of what it was like to be a parent. I couldn't get down to the shelter if anyone was still in the house, especially Mum with her in the family way.

Mum was running through the same emotions but it must have been worse for her. More kids were evacuated this time round than during the Blitz – Wally's school was like a ghost ship – so Mum was asked if she wanted to send us away. She said she'd consult the kids.

I was too old to qualify but Rosie, Wally and Peter all said no, just like I would have done. We all remembered what happened to Marjorie. What if we never came back?

With a new one on the way Mum was glad for the help

around the house. Whether that made up for the extra work it took to keep the young ones in check I'm not sure. Rosie did a lot of the work.

With my time on the roofs over I needed to find another job to pay my way. Once again it involved horses. And Euston. And *Wally*.

At home we were still scavenging around the demolition sites and roadworks for tarry blocks, old beds or anything we could throw on the fire when the weather turned later in the year. If a bomb hit our place there was so much timber inside it would burn for a month. Other people were able to afford coal and, while there was a demand, there had to be a supply.

Once again it was the stationmaster at Euston who came up with the job. There wasn't a person he didn't know and he said that one of the coal delivery boys had got ill. There was a horse and cart and route waiting if I fancied it. Helping Mr Smith out at thirteen years old I was considered a kid. At getting on for fifteen I was considered adult enough to do the work of men. Everyone grew up quickly back then.

The trains brought the coal and coke down from the north and, just like with the Savile Row supplies, we met it in the sidings. Unlike with the cloth, though, this was messy work. It was tipped out of the train carriage via a chute and onto a truck. Then I'd get a shovel and fill as many sacks as I had orders for and load my wagon.

All houses had a chute or a door where they wanted their coal or coke delivered so I'd knock on the front then tip a sack directly into their store. It was grubby work and the worst thing of all was cleaning the soot off in a measly five inches of water every night – and remembering Mr Davies every single time.

Wally asked if he could come out with me on my route so I took him a few times. While we were at the yard loading once, a train guard asked Wal if he'd like to earn a few shillings. Of course he did.

They gave him a broom and a shovel, then when the coal carriage had been unloaded he was sent inside to 'trim' it. It didn't matter how comprehensively you thought you'd emptied the car, there was always plenty tucked around the edges and in the corners. On a good day he'd fill a hundredweight sack and more than earn his shillings.

Like all little brothers, Wally was always trying to impress me. I pretended not to notice, just to have a bit of fun. Because coal was sold in smaller quantities the sacks were smaller and lighter and easier to lift. Coke, on the other hand, was a third taller. I could just about lift them and walk in a straight line. On Wal, they scraped the floor unless he scooped them over his back and shuffled along bent double. I kept giving him the coke to carry and waiting for him to fall over but he never did.

My route went all round King's Cross, Euston, Islington and Somers Town. Whether or not Mum had ordered any, she normally found a sack outside the door.

Pulling in thirty shillings a week was a big deal for me. Even after I'd given Mum half I still had plenty to spend. The problem was what to spend it on. I started going to the picture houses a bit more, and actually paying for a ticket. There was usually a girl with me by now so that made the time fly by a bit quicker. The old Luxe Theatre on Camden High Street had become the Plaza when I was young and was officially an Odeon by the time I took a friend in to see *Double Indemnity* or even one of the new Technicolor films like *National Velvet*.

Pubs became a bit of a draw as well. Dad didn't let me drink at home, even though I was working full time, but when I was out and about he couldn't stop me. After my coal round I'd tie my horse up outside a bar and go in for an ale and a bag of nuts for the horse. Normally the landlord wouldn't have someone as young as me in there on their own. Going in covered in soot, though, earned their respect. Nine times out of ten the landlord would serve me beer, no questions, like he would any other working man. Only the ones who knew Mum switched my order for lemonade. Respect for me was one thing. Fear of her was something else.

By the time the hopping season came around, I didn't need a note from Dr Shaw any more but I did need to ask for time off work.

I didn't get it.

'You're needed here.'

'I'm needed there as well. I always help.'

'Not this year, you don't. Men don't go hopping.'

We had a right falling out over that, me and the coal boss, but he wouldn't budge. I thought about telling him where to stick his smelly, dirty job but Mum wouldn't have it.

'If he says you're a man, do what the men do. Come down on Fridays.'

So that's what I did. Four o'clock Friday I was at London

Bridge with all the other working men, queuing for a ticket. Like them I also had a box of beers. If I was lucky I'd be able to get them stashed before Mum set eyes on them.

I'd been among adults all my life, from being a Pearly to working on the roofs, but I felt a fraud on that journey. These were real men. I could follow the conversations to a point and join in every so often. But then they'd go off down roads I just didn't know about, usually involving women, gambling or beer. I'd try and bluff then someone would look at me for the first time.

'Oi, tone it down, fellas, we've got a kid here. We don't want to give him ideas.'

Although some people worked in the fields on a Saturday, plenty took the weekend off to spend time with their menfolk. I got my fill of the family out of the way pretty soon, then after breakfast went off to fish. I couldn't believe it had been a whole year since I'd last been out there. But nothing had changed, at least not with the fish. When I got down to the lake, though, there were a couple of girls swimming. They called it swimming, anyway. I called it splashing around.

'You're gonna scare the fish away carrying on like that,' I said. 'Can't you go a bit deeper?'

'It's too dangerous,' one of them said.

'Course it's not. I'll show you.'

A few seconds later I was out in the middle of the lake, coaxing the girls with me, teaching them a few strokes on the way. All thought of fishing had fled my mind. I'd found a new reason to go hopping.

After dinner I met up with the girls in the woods. They

brought a blanket, I brought beer. It was the happiest night of my life until I got back to the hut. Mum and Dad were outside. The fire was virtually out so I knew it was late. Without its light it took me a moment to notice another fella standing with them.

'What have you done with my daughters?'

I guessed who he was talking about and shrugged. He came close but before he said anything else, caught a whiff of my breath.

'If you've been feeding my girls beer you'll have me to answer to.'

I protested my innocence, of course, but not all the words came out in the right order and the next morning I decided to get an earlier train.

Mixing alcohol with female company seemed like a good way to spend my spare time and money, but keeping it under the radar made it that bit more fun. The thrill of being caught by a girl's dad sneaking out of her house with a bottle or two made the beer taste that much nicer. Thanks to my fishing and exploring days, there wasn't a hidey-hole along the canal that I didn't know. We made little dens in sheds, tree stumps and even on a boat if it looked empty. Come May, however, and we had a whole city's worth of places to hang out as our Anderson shelters suddenly became unnecessary overnight.

It was 7 May 1945 and I'd already left the coal yard at Euston and was on my route. The first few stops went as normal, but when I turned off Upper Street I could see people coming out of their houses with smiles like Cheshire cats.

'What's going on?' I asked one woman.

'It's just been on the radio. Germany are going to surrender!'

'Blimey, when?'

'Tomorrow. But who can wait for then?' she said, and planted a wet smacker on my cheek.

A lot of us thought that the war would be over when news came out about the Führer taking his life a week earlier. When that didn't happen we all feared the worst. Japan were still out there, no one knew what Italy would do one day to the next, even after they'd surrendered in 1943, and Hitler's armies were still stationed all over Europe. And then there were the doodlebugs still fresh in the memory. Even if you never saw one, you could still see where they'd landed.

Every house I went to after that had an update. Tomorrow, people were saying, was going to be a national holiday. As soon as word came through from Germany. We just had to wait.

But who could wait? By the time I got back to the yard the beers were out. I might not have been allowed to go hopping but, the boss said, if he saw me the next day I'd be fired! Everyone was bubbling. In Somers Town the ladders were up against walls tying bunting, banners, balloons even, where they could be found, but mainly flags. Union Jacks, American Stars and Stripes – basically any scrap of cloth with a bit of red, white and blue in it was hung up.

The public holiday wasn't for another day but no work was done by anyone with a pulse. Without the official confirmation, though, we were in limbo and there was still a sense of unease as I went to bed. Was it over? Really? As I thought about it, I went over to the window and peered through the crack in my blackout board, expecting to see the moon and stars. Instead my eye was caught by a light across the street. *Hell*, I thought. *Someone should tell the baker's shop they've forgotten to pull down the shutters.*

Then I realised. They were doing it on purpose, weren't they? There wasn't much we could do to show the Nazis they were finished but tearing down our blackouts was a start. I grabbed at the card in my window and yanked it down. Out of habit I piled it neatly against the wall. Then, I realised, what was the point? Rosie came in while I was ripping it up.

'What are you doing?'

'We won't be needing these any more!'

Soon the whole place was illuminated like a lighthouse and we weren't alone. Even families who'd been heading off to bed, like me, stayed up just to shine their lamps into the night sky.

'We'll look proper fools if it's not over,' Mum said. But she was as happy with our little protest as everyone else.

Come the 8th of May we didn't know what to do with ourselves. By the time the official surrender came down the wire we'd been partying all day. No one was in their house for longer than it took to get another drink or a plate for some of the food people had magicked up in the street parties. I spent the morning on Chalton Street where the Coffee House had its doors open and the music from its 78rpm records blasting out. Other houses had their radios as loud as they'd go, and every hundred yards down the street there'd be a piano dragged out of someone's front room.

Even though I was with my family, there was somewhere else

I wanted to be. London for me had grown as I'd grown. I used to consider Somers Town as the be-all and end-all. Since I'd roamed further I'd got to know a bit more about the other boroughs. On a big celebration like this, I needed to be in the middle of things, and that meant hitting the West End.

I caught a tram as far as I could but the traffic meant it was quicker to walk. Even that was at a snail's pace. It didn't matter, though. It wasn't like the Coronation. There wasn't anything to miss if you were late. In any case, the mood of people milling towards Trafalgar Square was so buoyant it felt like a party already.

Pall Mall was chock-a-block. The King had played a blinder throughout the war, refusing to leave London and making it known he was living on rationed food and bath water like everyone else. When I heard a cheer rippling its way down towards Nelson's Column I guessed His Majesty must have put in an appearance on the balcony. There was a surge in the masses as we all tried to snatch a view but it was no good. Eventually I managed to get a leg on a lamppost and just caught a glimpse of two distant figures.

Whispers went round the crowds that the princesses, Elizabeth and Margaret, were milling among us, but I couldn't get within half a mile of where they probably were. In the end I gave up and started inching back through Admiralty Arch towards the square. That's when I saw her.

I don't know where she came from, but suddenly I saw a flash of long black hair whizz past me onto the floor. I stopped in my tracks to help the young woman up. She was about my age, maybe a bit older, and she was the most exotic person I'd ever seen.

'*Gracias* – thank you,' she said.

Beautiful and foreign!

'I'm Carmen,' she said.

'Pleased to meet you. I'm Johnny.'

I don't know where that came from. In that split second of meeting this lovely girl from another world, or so she seemed, my own life just didn't seem good enough. She wouldn't be interested in Boy-Boy or Alfie. She needed someone with a man's name.

It didn't hurt that almost every American film we saw at the Odeon had one Johnny or another in it, either as character or cast.

'Hello, Johnny,' she said in an accent that was as silky and soft as a rose petal. 'Perhaps you'd like to dance with me?'

All around Trafalgar Square there were pockets of grown-ups doing the hokey cokey. Carmen led us through a gap in the crowds and we joined in. It wasn't dancing that I recognised, but it was just about all I could manage.

No one wanted the day to end, me especially. I walked Carmen home to a little flat in Clerkenwell and promised to visit her on Saturday. Then I skipped on the back wheel of a truck and rode along the Farringdon Road to King's Cross, the happiest kid in the world.

Tuesday 8th of May was called VE Day to signify victory in Europe. We were still at war with Japan, as Churchill reminded the nation every night on the radio. We couldn't afford to let our guard down. But we did, we all did. I bet over at the War Office they had their feet up as well, at least for half the day.

Even though Japan was still out there resisting, like a lot of people, I thought that everything would change once the war was over. It didn't. The ration books stayed, the shortages didn't get any better and, worst of all, conscription wasn't stopped overnight. As a fifteen-year-old going on sixteen, this was creeping onto my radar. I wanted to see the world one day but not with a rifle in my hand. And definitely not with a bullet in my back. If I travelled, I wanted it to be with the people I loved and, right then, they were all living in NW1. I'd always been a family boy. The idea of leaving Mum and the others, even if we weren't fighting, was terrifying.

In any case, there was another person now who I wanted to see grow up. Mum had finally dropped and we had a lovely new addition to the Dole family: beautiful, bouncing Pauline. If she didn't round off our celebrations, what would? In fact, finally receiving word from David that he was alive and well – in Berlin! – topped it all, but my new sister was a pretty close second.

I also had Carmen to think about, something I was doing most of the time anyway. On our first date we just walked around her manor. She showed me a poster for a dance club in Farringdon and said we should go. I said I couldn't dance.

'I'll teach you.'

I confessed my problem to my dad who, surprisingly, had a solution.

'They're running dance classes down at the station on Euston Road. Every Thursday. Go and sign up.'

So I did. I felt a bit of a girl going in there but as soon as the stylus on the Phillips record player touched the shellac I was tapping my foot. The teacher there was an old professional who wanted to give something back to the boys who had risked their lives. With his help they could take their wives out and forget their problems for a few hours.

I loved it. Jive, waltz, cha-cha-cha – I had a go at them all. The only downside was there were no women there so we had to take it in turns going backwards or being twirled. But that was all right. We made sure we put the blackout blinds up, though.

I let Carmen give me a few lessons as well until I felt confident enough to cut a rug in her local hall or down at the Lyceum Theatre, which had been opened up for dancers during the war. I never thought anything could be so much fun.

Unfortunately, now it was safer to travel in Europe, Carmen's family moved out of London that summer. I'd never been heart-broken before but I think I was then. We had our last dance at the Royal Opera House. I only wish it had been on the stage. As we said goodbye I knew I would never fall in love again.

Within a few months of being born, Pauline was taken down to Paddock Wood for her first experience of country air. The kids took it in turns to look after her while Mum put in a shift in the fields. It was while they were away the news came through that Japan had finally given up. That really was it, this time. Even the most pessimistic politician had to admit the war was over.

I wished I'd been down there to celebrate with everyone else but that was the first year I didn't actually want to go. As much as I loved my family and my days around the lake, I'd found something I liked even more. *Someone*, I liked.

I'd found the girl I was going to marry.

18

It Was Your Beautiful Smile

Goodbye, Alfie. Hello, Johnny.

It had been a spur of the moment decision to call myself that when I met Carmen but as soon as it came out of my mouth I liked it. I felt different, more grown-up and more confident. No one at home called me Alfie anyway.

The Paramount on Tottenham Court Road was the best place for someone called Johnny to go. It's the Centre Point tower now, but the name lives on in the 'Paramount' restaurant at the top. I could be out of Chalton Street (where we were now living – another move) and down there in under twenty minutes if I hung on to the back of the right cab. On a good night I wouldn't have soot in my ears but once the lights went down inside who could tell?

I was happy to go on my own but if one of my mates from the coal run or a neighbour was up for a jive then all the better, if only because it worked out cheaper. A game of rock, paper, scissors on the way decided who would pay to get in and who would go round the back to wait to be let in through the trades-man's entrance. Some nights I'd open the door and a dozen other blokes with the same plan would pile in, sometimes with their dates. I always drew a line at that. If a girl knows you don't think she's worth paying for, you'll lose her to the first fella who foxtrots her way.

Even though the odd house had a record player, there weren't any discos. On the stage at the Paramount every Saturday we had a five-piece band. Sometimes a singer would get up but usually they'd belt through the instrumental numbers. When the band stopped for a break, that's when you got to sit down. Ideally next to a girl who'd caught your eye.

Carmen had been gone about a month and I was enjoying myself on the dance floor with a crowd of older girls – ladies, I suppose – one night. The band had been going all-out to get us worn out with one jive followed by a jitterbug – the new craze from America – after another, and the whole room was on their feet. All except one woman who was nursing a drink at a table by the side. Even though she wasn't dancing with anyone she didn't look lonely or unhappy. In fact, I didn't think I'd ever seen a more beaming smile. As soon as the dance finished I thanked my partner and went over.

'Hello, my dear,' I said. 'My name's Johnny. What's your name?'

'Oh hello, Johnny,' the woman said. 'You can call me Edna.'

'Is that your name?'

'Yes,' she laughed.

'Then that's what I will call you.'

I offered to buy her a drink but she was okay.

'Why weren't you dancing?' I asked.

For the first time her smile flickered.

'Ah, this old thing,' she said, and tapped her left leg. 'I've got polio. I can't move like the rest of you.'

'So why do you come, then?' I was a bit blunt.

'Because I love the music,' she said, her smile back as bright as before. 'No one can stop me dreaming.'

We chatted for the next ten minutes and she had me in fits. Normally it was me with the jokes, but Edna was a sharp one. Still, even she was lost for words when the band struck up again for another round of jives and I said, 'Come on, then, let's take a turn.'

She looked sad. 'I told you, I can't jitterbug. It's too fast for me.'

'Well, can you waltz?'

She nodded.

'Then let's waltz!'

I helped her to her feet and, the pair of us giggling, we walked on to the dance floor. Everyone was flying around, feet and elbows flaying, but I found us a spot in the middle and then with my hands on her shoulders and waist, I picked up the beat of the band and started to sway. We didn't say a word for the whole song. As far as I was concerned, it was everyone else dancing at the wrong speed. By the end of it a few people had even stopped to watch us. When we parted at the end there was even some applause.

Even going slowly, Edna could only manage a few dances before needing a rest. When I sat next to her she said, 'Don't be daft. You came here to dance, so dance.'

'Actually, I came here to meet you.'

'Ha! Well, you've done that. Go and dance with someone else and see me later.'

I couldn't imagine another girl sending me off to dance with someone else. That was another tick for this one.

Afterwards we walked outside, yapping away.

'Why did you come over to me, Johnny? You saw I was crippled,' Edna asked. 'You could have had your pick of girls.'

'It was your beautiful smile, Edna,' I said. 'Never stop smiling.'

We gassed so much I didn't notice for a while how much it hurt her to walk. We caught a bus together over to Holborn and as she got off she said, 'See you next Saturday?'

'You try and stop me. But next week I'll pick you up.'

I'm not having you walking more than you have to.

The following Saturday she was surprised to see me standing on her doorstep. Her parents were pretty taken aback too. They'd have been more shocked if they'd seen how I got there. Edna didn't twig until she'd almost walked past the large blue lorry parked on her street.

'Aren't you coming with me?' I called out.

I watched her look at me, then the truck, then back again to me.

'In this? Are you serious? Where did you get it?'

'It belongs to a neighbour,' I said. Which was true. Only the neighbour had no idea I'd borrowed it for the night. He was in the Eastnor Castle as usual and wouldn't be in a state to notice anything by morning.

'Can you even drive?'

'I learned on the way here.'

'Johnny Dole, what are we going to do with you?'

'Anything you want, Edna. Now let me help you in.'

The cab was so high I had to give her a leg up. We managed it so she didn't look too unladylike climbing in. Then I went round the front, wound the crankshaft, and hopped in before it conked out.

'Fares please!' I said, laughing, and we bunny-hopped our way across the city.

The Paramount was famous at the time for its open-door policy. It didn't matter what your nationality was, or your colour, if you wanted a good time you were welcome to find it there. With the war over, American troops in large numbers on the lookout for fun discovered the Paramount. Among them was the odd African-American. Nobody in the Paramount looked twice but not everyone was so open-minded. Sometimes there was a bit of bother with the police outside. After what we'd all just been through I couldn't believe anyone would want to pick a fight with a man because of his race.

The Americans were good to have around. I met a couple on my coal round who were willing to pay for a bit of coke in stockings, cigarettes and sugar, among other things. That suited me. It wasn't hard to find buyers for anything like that and I quickly earned more than the price of a sack.

Wally liked them being here as well. On Bonfire Night I took him out to Oxford Street to hang around outside the clubs and restaurants there. His face was blacked with shoe polish, he was wearing rags and I had a sign saying, 'Penny for the guy'. I don't think a single US soldier passed without throwing him a couple of coins. It was the most money he'd ever earned.

At sixteen I still wasn't legally allowed to drink in pubs unless it was with food. Even then we still weren't allowed to order for ourselves, although if you looked around you'd find someone willing to turn a blind eye on a slow night.

On my own, though, I had no shortage of people willing to buy me a pint. Friday night in Camden was not a place for the faint-hearted as the pay-day drinkers hit the bars. A lot of Irish navvies over to help with the rebuilding liked to have a jar or two in the Bedford Arms, tucked inside the Bedford theatre building on the high street. The theatre put on a lot of good musicals and plays. Peter Sellers used to live upstairs when his mum was on the stage there. But on a Friday night the biggest show in town was the Irishmen. With a few pence in their pocket, they'd start the night queuing for the telephone to tell their families how well they were doing.

'I'm doing wonderfully, Mother. Lord Macmillan hired me personally.'

'I can't tell you what I'm doing, Dad, but I can tell you the King's happy with my work.'

They all tried to outdo each other. By the end of the night they were almost believing their own stories. Arguments would start, and they'd get louder and louder until, usually, the Black Marias (police vans) would be queuing up out the front to take them away for the night.

Another Camden character was Lord Honolulu. He called himself an African prince and maybe he was. He was flash enough with his colourful suit and feathers sticking out of his hat. He said he liked coming into sawdust-on-the-floor boozers to meet 'real' people. In fact, I think it was to rip us off.

Lord Honolulu was into the racing. He claimed to own a stable of horses and have the inside steer on all the big races. He'd come bowling in shouting, 'I've got an 'orse, I've got an 'orse, come and have a bet.'

If you paid him five shillings he'd give you a tip for the race. According to him, it was nailed on, a dead cert. Only an act of God would stop it coming through.

'Keep this tip to yourself,' he'd say, 'or the odds will come down!'

What I didn't realise until years later was that if there were ten runners and ten people asking, he'd tell them all a different horse without anyone knowing. He looked a clown but he was canny, the old prince, and one of the true characters.

Our house in Chalton Street had a basement level that you looked down into from the street. There were steps running down and a little passageway there called an 'airy'. It was a great place to hide and leap out in front of Wally's little pals. You also had a cracking view of ladies' legs as they walked by.

We had a sewer problem one day where a pipe had been weakened by a bomb blast and just gave way. A lot of waste made its way to the surface so that put the airy out of bounds for a while until it was drained and fixed. I was surprised Mum put up with it. Considering how many times we'd moved already, and sometimes for no reason I could make out, I thought this would have her packing up again in a shot. But she liked the house. We had it all to ourselves and we'd only just settled, so she put up with it. Unfortunately, it nearly cost one of our family her life.

It was a hot day so Mum had put Pauline's cot over by the open window in the basement. She had the curtains drawn so my sister could get a breeze without the sunlight while she slept. She'd done it dozens of times. There was no need even to stay in the room with Pauline. She'd soon sing out when she was awake.

On this particular day I'd been out and about. When I arrived home, sun beating down on my back, I could see a strange fella leaning over the railings on top of our airy. Something about him didn't look right. He was shifty, to say the least.

I called out, 'Can I help you?' and he span round, fear etched on his face.

'Look,' he said.

Down on the windowsill there was a rat the size of a cat. It was big, dirty and black and it was making its way along the ledge to where the curtains parted in the middle.

'It looks like it can smell something behind those curtains,' the man said.

'I don't know what,' I said. 'That's my house and I know there's no food in that room.'

Then I realised what was there.

Pauline!

I jumped down the steps making as much noise as I could. It was still sludgy at the bottom and I nearly went arse over tit, which meant I had to make a grab for the railings. It wasn't pretty but it was enough to disturb the rat. It took one look at my arms and legs flailing all over the place then dived under the steps into the coal shed.

Dad got a couple of his friends round later and they smoked it out. It was decided it must have come up through the sewers when the pipe burst and had hidden out in the shed. It was pretty much nocturnal, so for it to have ventured out in such bright daylight must have required some temptation – and the smell of milk on a baby's vest was just the temptation it needed. When Dad brought the dead rodent out we held it up against the cot. It was probably the same size as Pauline. No one knew what it would have done to her but we all agreed it wouldn't have been nice.

You make your own luck, my granddad used to say, but that has its limits when you're as young as Pauline. What could she have done against a giant sewer rat? Beyond eating, sleeping and burping, she couldn't do much full stop.

The same could be said of Arthur, my old coal horse. I loved the old boy but he wasn't treated right by the yard owners. Not how I would have treated him if he were mine, and not how Kitty was treated by Granddad.

I had an argument with my boss one day about the sores on Arthur's legs. They needed attention, I said. The vet on Royal College Street would be able to sort him out.

'It'd be cheaper to shoot him,' the boss said. 'Get on with your route and leave my animals to me.'

The man was older than Dad and about twice my weight. There was nothing I could do except load my cart and set out for the day. I'd barely got up the Pentonville Road when I realised there *was* something I could do. I pulled over and led Arthur into the grounds of the chapel. It's Joseph Grimaldi Park now. There was a nice bit of turf there for the horse to nibble on and the church gave enough shade for him to be comfortable. I looped his reins around the gate post and unhooked the barrow.

'There you go, Arthur. You have a nice day off. I know I'm going to.'

Then I walked over to Holborn to call for Edna. When I walked back that night Arthur had been picked up and, I suppose, a lot of people on the Pentonville Road wouldn't need to buy coke for a while.

I didn't tell Dad that I'd just walked away from my job but he found out soon enough when the boss came round shouting the odds. It wasn't Dad's nature to let someone shout at his family, even when he agreed with them, so he told the guy to sling his hook before he had it slung for him. Then he shouted at me instead, which I suppose was fair. When he'd calmed down he said he knew of a job with a builder's crew. Thirty shillings a week and I'd have to give Mum half as usual.

'Deal.'

That wasn't the only change in my life, but it was one of the more positive ones.

*

It was a sad day in Somers Town when Granddad announced that he'd worn his Pearly suit for the last time.

'The world's changed,' he said. 'It's not the same any more. Everyone needs help, not just the hospitals, and it'll take more than a few buttons to put things straight.'

I'd never thought about him retiring – or abdicating. But, thinking about it, we hadn't been out as a team for a year or so and he had only been doing bits and bobs when people asked him for a favour. The last time I'd seen him in his buttons was on VE Day. Even then he'd stayed more in the background than usual. For the first time I had to entertain the possibility that he was just getting old. He was nearly seventy. Maybe the war had taken more of a toll on him than anyone realised.

'Does that make Dad King now?' I asked.

'It would if he wanted it,' Granddad said. 'But he and Annie are thinking along the same lines as me. Our time has gone. It's a young man's business.' He paused. 'And you're a young man . . .'

So that was it: seventeen years after he'd carried Henry Croft's coffin, Granddad was drawing a line for himself under the road-sweeper's legacy.

I thought about carrying on single-handed like he'd said. Granddad was right. The Pearlies had been started by a teenager even younger than me. *I should do it*. But the idea of being a Pearly without Granddad there to lead the charge made me feel sick with worry. And not only that, he was the inspiration in Somers Town and had been since Henry had died. People looked up to him. No one looked up to me.

I was so thrown by Granddad's announcement that the next time I saw Edna she knew something was up.

'I've got something to show you,' I said, and pulled out a box. Inside was my last Pearly suit. It didn't fit me any more, but I'd grown out of them before and just made a new one. This was the first time I'd even considered not upgrading.

Edna had heard about the buttons but never seen me wearing them.

'What do you want to do?' she asked when I'd told her my dilemma.

'I don't know,' I said, 'but I don't think I can do it without Dad and Granddad.'

'What will they say?'

'I don't know about Dad but I know Granddad will be devastated. He started something special and he wants me to carry it on.'

'But?'

'But I can't. I don't know how to tell him, but I can't do it any more. I've got my own life to lead – with you.'

'Don't you blame me, Johnny. If you want to be a Pearly, you be a Pearly.'

'I don't think I do any more,' I finally admitted.

Dad felt the same. To be a King you need to have something about you. We didn't have it. Telling Granddad was one of the hardest conversations of my life. I'd made him angry plenty of times before but never disappointed. He was now.

Another change, an even worse one if that was possible, came on the eve of my eighteenth birthday. We'd just had Christmas and New Year and everyone was on the mend after a brutal few years. My relationship with Edna was stronger than ever and we'd even discussed the future. I knew that she was going to be part of mine.

But the future was something I didn't have any say over. At the start of January I got the letter I'd been dreading ... I was being called up. My two years of compulsory national service would start at the end of the month. I was going to join the army.

The station was packed. Every square inch of the concourse at Waterloo had the same scene being played out. Young men, in their Sunday best, were standing surrounded by crying women and children, and stern-faced men. I was no exception, except my send-off party was larger than most. Mum and Dad were there, David was back, Walter, Rosie, Peter and even baby Pauline lined up alongside them. Behind them, Granddad and Grandma were managing to keep it together. We all knew that the country was no longer at war but no one had happy thoughts about the army. We'd lost thousands of good men and women as a nation. I was being shipped to Aldershot with the other fresh-faced lads to be prepared to make the ultimate sacrifice.

I smiled at them all as bravely as I could and wondered what was going to happen to the family now without Granddad leading from the front with his buttons. What, in fact, was going to happen to our little patch of London town?

I could think about that on the train. For now, there was one other person there and she was clinging to me like her life depended on it.

'I'll be home soon enough, Edna, I promise.'

'No, you won't,' she said. 'You'll be there at least six months without leave. That's what the letter said.'

'I'll find a way,' I winked. 'Even if I have to borrow a tank.'

Milling around on the platform were a dozen men in army uniform. They all had clipboards, which brought back bad memories of being evacuated. I wondered yet again why Marjorie had decided not to come back with us. I would never stop wondering that. As the soldiers began corralling us onto the special army train, I made my final round of hugs. My last kiss was to Edna, but I saved my final words for the old man with the moustache. I hadn't planned them, they just came to me out of the blue as I was halfway down the platform. I stopped walking to the train, turned and heard the curses of a dozen emotional men who now had to shuffle around me. I didn't care. I needed to speak.

'Granddad!' I called out. 'When I come home, I'm going to be Pearly King!'

His face transformed before my eyes and I swear his coughing was to hide the tears.

'Just you do that, Alfie Dole,' he shouted back. 'And I'll be here to crown you.'

I was actually smiling as I boarded the train. Whatever the next weeks, months and years had in store, my days as the Pearly *Prince* of St Pancras were coming to an end . .

Epilogue

Can I Have A Chip, Dave?

Well, I kept my word – to both of them. Sort of.

All the tea in the China could not keep me away from Edna. I lasted five weeks in Hampshire before I saw a truck leaving for London so I bribed the driver with a nice bit of fish and then I hopped on. I couldn't go directly to Edna's because her parents would have been furious at me doing a bunk. But I got word to her and she came round to our house. We had a wonderful twenty-four hours before there was a knock on the door. I knew who it would be before Wally told me.

'It's a couple of military coppers, Alf. They said you shouldn't be here.'

It's true I might not have been completely honest about how I'd got there.

'I'll sort it out,' I said, grabbing my coat as I walked. 'I'll see you soon, Wal.' Then I went round the family saying my good-byes, promising Edna I wouldn't leave it so long next time.

'But . . .'

'Trust me,' I said. 'I'll be back.'

By now the two MPs were standing in the doorway.

'Are you coming, Dole, or do we need to arrest you?'

'I'm coming, I'm coming,' I said. 'I just need to stop off and buy a nice bit of fish.'

At least once a month I made it back to the Old Oak (the Smoke), arriving with a shopping list of whatever bribe I'd promised my getaway driver. Once the MPs realised I just wanted a break and I wasn't trying to abscond from national service, they left it later and later to pick me up. I think that way they got a nice little breather as well. But they always knew where to find me.

Almost always.

One weekend they waited at the house for ages, knocked on Granddad's door and searched all known relatives. Even Edna's parents were paid a call. But each visit from the officers drew a blank. No one was in. I don't know if it was inspiration or they were just thirsty, but they wound up in the Eastnor Castle – which just happened to be where we all were.

'Come on, Alfie, time to go,' one of them said.

'You wouldn't ruin a man's honeymoon, would you?' I asked.

'Who's got married?'

'Me!'

I got back to Aldershot even later that night.

*

Sadly, things between me and Edna didn't work out. I take the blame. To make ends meet after conscription I enlisted in the Merchant Navy. I may as well have just applied for a divorce because the result was the same. Getting back from a ship berthed off the Gold Coast of Australia is a damn sight harder than bunking a ride home from Hampshire, so the distance between us as a couple grew with each month I was away. But it wasn't just us two affected. We'd had a son, Patrick, but as I fell out of contact with Edna, I never got to know him. Every day that passed I thought of him and what he would he would be like. But as weeks turned into months, and months into years, I knew that my time had gone. As much as I wanted to, I couldn't just go waltzing back into his life after years of not being there. That wouldn't be fair on him.

No, I'd made my bed. I had to lie in it. But if I could have done one thing in my life differently . . .

I never stopped thinking about Patrick and the life he might be leading. But when I met the lovely Lizzie in 1953 and had four wonderful children – Philip, Diane, Jimmy and Gary – I knew that I had the chance to do things differently. No more running away, I would be there for my family.

So, I thought, *what did I like most about being a kid?*

The answer took me about a second.

Hopping.

That's what I'll do with my kids.

The farm we used to stay on had shut down by the time I took Lizzie, Phil and Di down there, but there was another one in

Paddock Wood that looked just like it. As soon as I stepped into the field, I was transported back to the 1930s. The huts were the same, the fireplace was the same, the people were the same.

It didn't take long for the kids to settle in doing exactly the same things I used to: a bit of hopping in the mornings followed by swimming, climbing, exploring – generally making themselves scarce and enjoying not being in the city – in the afternoons. I loved seeing them having fun – especially as I got to do it seven days a week, unlike my old man. The only downside to my days there as a kid was Dad not being around during the week. I solved that by getting employed as a tractor driver. I'd be there for as long as the kids.

In fact, I was there longer. Each year we went down we got there earlier and left later. When the season was over, I still couldn't bring myself to leave the fields. Only the kids' education got me into the car. But even as we pulled out of the farm, I'd be looking in the rear view mirror until the huts were out of sight. During winter, if Lizzie couldn't find me, she knew where I'd be: shivering in a hut, just enjoying the stillness of the countryside.

Some years I couldn't wait for the hopping season to get started, so I'd drag the family down to the farm gate the second the school holidays started. That way we could get a little holiday in before the work began. It didn't always go to plan.

One year the farmer came out and said, 'Alf, what are you doing here? The huts are being hosed down. They won't be ready yet for another couple of days.'

'Can we still use the field?'

'Course you can.'

So we made our fire, we swam and laughed – all as normal. Then, at the end of the day, we all piled into my little car and slept in there. Anything to be in the country.

I became such a regular down at the farm that I knocked through two huts and installed a small bathroom and kitchen. We ended up with a place nicer than our flat! Even when the farm stopped hiring for hop helpers years later, we continued to go down there just for the holiday. And, when Granddad, Dad and Mum used to come and visit, the whole world just got better.

Every minute spent not in the countryside cast a bit of shadow over my life but, as I kept telling myself, as long as I didn't have to go away to work we were doing all right.

It meant taking some rum old jobs. With my background in the Royal Electrical and Mechanical Engineers I got a job in a white goods shop, but being stuck behind a counter all day didn't inspire me, so I began selling vacuum cleaners door to door in the Angel area of north London. When I got the job my boss said something curious: 'Do not stray from your streets or there'll be trouble.'

He didn't tell me what kind.

I was having no luck one day when I decided to try a new patch over Hackney way. The housewives there snapped up the chance to buy a new Hoover, especially when I let them pay on the strap. Apparently the boys who sold stuff in their area didn't accept weekly instalments, one woman told me.

'Well, you're dealing with a professional now, love,' I said. 'They sound like amateurs.'

I celebrated a good day's work with a few frames in a billiard hall off Bethnal Green Road. I was just about to break when I got a tap on the shoulder.

'Are you the geezer selling vacuum cleaners?' a gorilla of a bloke asked.

I looked at my suitcase by the bar covered in Hoover stickers.

'Not me, squire,' I said, hoping the bloke couldn't read.

It turned out he could.

He took the cue off me and snapped it in two. Then he led me out into the corridor where a mate was waiting.

'Who sent you?' the mate asked.

'Sent me where?'

'Onto our turf.'

'I don't know what you're talking about.' I genuinely didn't. What's more, I was beginning to think I didn't want to know.

The big guy put his hand around my throat and pushed me up against the wall.

'This is the Krays' territory,' he said. 'No one hawks stuff round here without their say so.'

'Well, why didn't you mention it . . .?'

It turned out they'd only heard about me because of the good terms I'd been offering. The Krays didn't let you pay on the never-never, so obviously customers preferred my deals. If I'd charged full whack they might never have got wind of me.

That was my only brush with 'the Firm' but the Krays continued to haunt me. I was in Manchester the following year and two coppers pinned me to the wall outside a boozer.

'Reggie Kray, you're under arrest!'

'I'm not Reggie Kray!' I said. But when they showed me the warrant picture even I could see the similarities. Big nose, sharp suit, Italian style good looks – an honest mistake!

I retired from the Hoover game soon after my run-in at the billiard hall but travelling and working still appealed. When I saw an ad for bus drivers I applied and got taken on. That didn't last long either. The problem started when I was driving the number 45 north to south one day and saw my old mum walking in the rain. I pulled over and said, 'Where are you off to, Mum?'

'Home.'

'Hop on.'

'The 45 doesn't go anywhere near our house.'

'It does now!'

I drove her straight home to the soundtrack of a dozen angry passengers dinging the bell.

Not surprisingly, I was soon looking for another gig and, when a lovely old gypsy knife grinder called Tom Dyton asked me to drive his lorry while he sharpened blades in the back, I leapt at it. When he passed on, I kept the business going, taking Di, Gary and the others out with me. It was a nice little family concern for a while. But, as lovely as it was earning a crust, getting a bit of fresh air and spending time with the kids in the process, I couldn't help feeling there was something missing from my life.

Then, in 1981, I realised what it was.

I've always liked a bit of wheeling and dealing. I get that from my grandfather. He never made a bad deal but he never conned anyone either. He just liked the process of moving things on. I dabbled a bit with cars, boot sales and all sorts, and it was while I was selling motors that I ran into a good old friend of mine called Arthur Warwick. As well as being a straight-up bloke, Arthur spent a lot of his spare time collecting for charity around the pubs and halls of southeast London. At first, when he told me that, I thought he was pulling my leg. Car dealers have always had a bit of a spiv reputation, so who could blame me?

But when he told me what he wore I knew he wasn't winding me up.

'I'm the Pearly King of Sydenham, Alf,' he said. 'Didn't you know?'

'No, I didn't, Arthur. And I've met my share of Pearlies.'

Over a few ales I told him my story – of Dad, of Granddad, and our links to Henry Croft. At the end of it Arthur said, 'Why don't you pick your family buttons up, Alf? You're more entitled than any of us.'

'I don't know, Arthur. I think my time in buttons has gone.'

I anguished over it all night and on the journey home. Was I making the right decision? Was there a place for Pearlies in the 1980s? I was living with my new partner at the time, a lovely woman I'd met on the dance floor – again! – called Mary. When I got into bed that night I woke her up. 'Mary,' I said, 'how would you like to become a Queen?'

'Alfie Dole, have you been drinking?'

'Yes, I have but I'm not drunk. In fact, I've never been so clear-headed.'

'What are you talking about?'

'I'm going to honour a promise I made to my granddad,' I said. 'I'm finally going to become a Pearly King.'

I made two suits. One a 'smother', covered in buttons. Another less flashy with a few lines of mother-of-pearl here and there. One had the emblem of a fish, another a ship, both representing my time in the navy and the seafood stalls my granddad and I ran. I also sewed a circle on each to represent family and the circle of life. When Gary and Diane decided to become Pearly Prince and Princess of St Pancras, I couldn't have been prouder. But I found myself wondering, I wish I could have asked Patrick as well. The problem was, I had no idea where he was and no clue how to contact him or his mother.

The plan was to ease myself into being a Pearly again but the first time I stepped out in the suit I felt like a new man. I couldn't believe how I'd gone so many years without wearing it. All the old patter, the songs, the spoons playing – the sheer sense of devilment that was always in me – just came flooding back. I walked into my local pub in Plumstead and within ten minutes there was a sing-song going on and we'd raised a hundred quid for charity. And not just any old charity. Granddad had always supported Great Ormond Street Hospital, so that was who was going to get the contents of my tins as well.

For all the good I did with my suit, I have to admit it did a lot for me too. I'd forgotten what it was like to walk into a room and have all eyes on me, waiting for me to tell a yarn or sing a few bars of a bawdy ditty. After so many years of drifting from one job to another I realised that this was what I'd always wanted to do. What I'd been born to do.

Other people agreed. I started getting invites to functions all over London. I was guest of honour every year at Leadenhall Market for St George's Day and another one of their regulars, Boris Johnson, always hunted me out when he was there.

'All right, your Highness?' he'd say.

'Hello there, Boris. Have you come to ask my help fixing London again?'

In 2010, when he was on the campaign trail for the Conservative Party, he introduced me to his mate David Cameron. I don't think the Tory leader had met anyone like me before, but I do know that when he wanted a tenner for some chips I lent it to him. Of course, as soon as he had his cod in batter, I was straight over.

'Can I have a chip, Dave?'

It's not just politicians who like to have a bit of Pearly contact. Over the years I've had many, many celebrities just come up to me while I've been out and about, wanting to have their picture taken with a Pearly King and to ask me about the heritage. I'm not hard to spot. As well has having buttons on my suits, I bought a black cab and covered that in stickers of red, white and blue buttons. So, not only is it Pearly, it's patriotic as well. Maybe that's why I was asked to escort Dame Vera Lynn to The War and Peace Show in Kent a few years ago.

Every Sunday I drive down to Greenwich Market and park up

on the double yellows so tourists and traders can come over for a photo in exchange for a few pence in the collection tin. I'm a fixture there. So much so, I was invited to appear in the gangland movie *Honest* a few years ago, playing myself. The producers wanted a bit of authentic London and they got it.

I love meeting people, famous or not. Yes, it gives me a thrill when Barbara Windsor phones me up from time to time but – and don't tell Babs this – I'm just as happy sitting next to an old biddy at a bus stop and waiting with her till her bus comes along or popping into primary schools to have a chat with the kids in assemblies.

But, I have to be up front, getting the invite from our old pal Suggs to jump up on stage with his band, Madness, at the Hackney Empire a few years ago was pretty special. They're all great London lads, so it was a privilege for me and Diane to give them all Pearly caps and honorary titles. We've played with them loads of times since, including a few gigs at Vicky Park in front of tens of thousands of people. Granddad would have been so proud!

It's thanks to my Pearly Princess, Diane that we went all upmarket a few years ago and got a website, Pearlies.org.uk, to advertise our availability for charity work. After all, meeting rock stars and actresses is all very nice, but it's fundraising that we do best. A lot of sweet people have used the site to contact Diane but, in 2009, she got a call that changed all our lives.

'Hello,' a young lady's voice said. 'This might sound a daft question but is your dad's middle name Avory?'

'Yes, it is,' Diane replied. 'Why?'

'Because I think he's my granddad.'

I have so much to thank my Pearly heritage for, but the fact it helped my son Patrick track me down after sixty years was the greatest gift of all. Diane arranged a meet-up and we had a tearful reunion. But even on the way I didn't dare get my hopes up too much in case it wasn't true. But one glance at the face staring back at me told me I was looking at my son. Patrick was the spitting image of me as a younger man. In fact, when he'd first been shown my picture online, he'd said, 'Well, now I know what I'm going to look like when I'm older.'

Not only did I find a son, but I got two brilliant new grandchildren in Andrea and Justin, and four great-grandchildren. On top of that, Di, Gary, Philip and Jimmy all got another brother.

And St Pancras got a whole new line in its Pearly dynasty. Lee, my grandson, is now the new Pearly King.

Sadly, Alf passed away in May 2013, shortly after telling his life story. Meanwhile, Alf's daughter, Diane, has been keeping the family's Pearly tradition very much alive and has been joined by her son, Alf's grandson, Lee, who is now the fifth generation Pearly King of St Pancras.

Jeff Hudson, April 2014

Afterword by Diane Gould, Alf's daughter, and Pearly Princess of St Pancras

Alf's family and friends are so fortunate to be left with the many fun and uplifting memories of someone who always maintained a positive and enthusiastic attitude to life; someone who would not be affected by what others might see as mistakes or failure. Out of this attitude came a boundless energy for life.

As Dad has recalled, the tradition of hopping in Kent was a mainstay in our family life. Our annual visits to the hop fields near Paddock Wood in Kent were wonderful times, playing in the outdoors, away from the Smoke. We'd hear stories from friends and relatives and listen to Dad playing the spoons and singing songs. The strong sense of community and the magic of the countryside during those trips helped us get through many of the challenges life would throw at us later.

After seeing and experiencing so much through the wartime years, followed by his time in the National Service, he managed to bring his Cockney cheer to far-flung corners of the world during his time in the Merchant Navy.

Dad always kept his hand in fixing things and he became the king of recyclers. In his later years he could regularly be found at boot sales, where inevitably there was much merriment from his singing and banter. He loved seeing people happy and was always ready to lend a hand to those in need. He was forever willing to come to the aid of the underdog and champion their cause, and I think this was because he knew what suffering was. It was the same whether it was his family members or the seriously ill children at Great Ormond Street Hospital whom he visited on Christmas Day.

Like many a man of his era, living through the tough times of the 1930s and '40s, Dad did not always find it easy to express his love in ways those closest to him could understand. Somehow, though, his love was always clear when singing a song. In his final few days, when he was stoically facing his own death, he sang a new song to me:

> *'You've got to live and let live if you want to get by,*
> *It's only a matter of time until you die,*
> *What difference does it make if you're rich or if you're broke?*
> *In a hundred years from now it will all be a joke.*
> *Don't kick a man when he's down,*
> *Give him a real handshake.*
> *If you're not rewarded then what difference does it make?*
> *You've got to learn how to live if you want to get by,*
> *So I say live and let live, not live and let die.'*

Thanks, Dad, your passion for life and care for others will live on.

Acknowledgements

There were many, in addition to his loving family who loyally supported Dad and what he represented over the years. I would like to mark our special appreciation of the following people:

Lyndsey Burke, the fund-raising co-ordinator at Great Ormond Street Hospital for many years, who sent this message when Dad passed:

'Alf was a very special person to me. For the past ten years he visited me every month, pressed £100 into my hand "for the children" and we'd have a good old natter. When I left Great Ormond Street, it was hard saying goodbye to so many wonderful donors who had become such good friends. Alf was one of those people whom everyone loved. There is a hole left in the world without him.'

Jimmy O'Gara, one of our most loyal supporters, recognising the shared London roots of the Pearlies of St Pancras and the band Madness, and enabling Alf's and others' input into their theatrical concerts.

Chas Hodges and Dave Peacock. Dad was always singing

Chas & Dave's songs to his impromptu audiences, augmented with his quick-fingered playing of the spoons on his regular outings around the streets of Greenwich. He especially enjoyed the occasions when we joined up with these 'Kings of Rockney' in person to have a proper Cockney knees-up!

Rex Cadman and Georgina Martin, and their team at the 'War and Peace Revival' who kindly provided the perfect space for Dad to be in his element, entertaining the crowds and raising fun and funds in his own imitable way.

Pearly King Jimmy Jukes and Pearly Queen Michelle Thorpe, along with their 'UK Homes 4 Heroes' team, who have provided us with great Pearly cameraderie and loyal support over the years.

James 'Pieman' Thurston, our good friend, who provides the best pie 'n mash around, and keeps us Pearlies well fed in proper authentic manner.

There were three special ladies in Dad's life. Following on from Edna was my mum Lizzy and finally Mary, with whom he forged a great partnership for the last 25 years of his life.

Finally, on behalf of Dad, I would like to express our gratitude to Susan Smith, of MBA Literary Agents, and writer Jeff Hudson. For many years Dad had talked about a book, making various attempts to start writing it, so when Susan made contact Dad was more than ready to give Jeff a marathon ride through the old times. As it turned out, their sessions together in early 2013 were just in the nick of time, as Dad passed away on 13 May of that year.